Wild Thing

The author with Smokey and Bongo, on the Upper Selway. *Wes Rose photo.*

Wild Thing

Backcountry Tales and Trails

STACY GEBHARDS

Washington State University Press
Pullman, Washington

Washington State University Press
P.O. Box 645910
Pullman, Washington 99164-5910
Phone: 800-354-7360   FAX: 509-335-8568
Email: wsupress@wsu.edu
www.publications.wsu.edu/wsupress

Cover photographs courtesy of the author.
Illustrations in the book are by the author.

Library of Congress Cataloging-in-Publication Data

Gebhards, Stacy V.
       Wild thing : backcountry tales and trails / Stacy Gebhards.
            p.   cm.
       ISBN 0-87422-182-X
       1. Gebhards, Stacy V. 2. Idaho. Dept. of Fish and Game—Officials
and employees Biography. 3. Wildlife management—Idaho Anec-
dotes. 4. Outdoor life—Humor. I. Title.
       SK354.G43A3   1999
       796.5'092—dc21
       [B]   99-16216
                                                                         CIP

Dedication

To Maria, Barb, Sandy, Judi, and John, who joined me on many backcountry trips and also waited patiently at home on many others while Dad was off in the mountains.

Acknowledgements

Without the companionship of those who shared these adventures with me, including the mules and horses, there would be no stories to tell. Thanks also to the Idaho Department of Fish and Game for permission to utilize photos and materials previously published in the Department's magazine, *Idaho Wildlife*.

Contents

Preface: Wild Thing xi

One: The Search 1

Two: Out West, Somewhere 9

Three: River of No Return 17

Four: High Mountain Trout 27

Five: Encounters Number Eight and Nine 33

Six: Blue Lights on Whitewater 37

Seven: The Sound of Music and Politicians 41

Eight: Rivers, Rattlers, and Floating Rocks 49

Nine: Cookbook Mountain 57

Ten: Backcountry Citizenry 75

Eleven: Beaver Fever 79

Twelve: Winter Secrets 83

Thirteen: The Lenticulars are Coming 99

Fourteen: Saddles and Sores 103

Afterword: The Missing Piece 127

About the Author 129

Bruneau Canyon, July 1973. *Stacy Gebhards photo; courtesy Idaho Department of Fish and Game.*

Preface | Wild Thing

HIDDEN SOMEWHERE WITHIN our complex genetic puree of molecules, DNA, genes, chromosomes, and whatever else is in the recipe, is an ingredient I call the Wild Thing. It is made up of survival and social skills that have persisted in humans and animals over millions of years, allowing for evolution of the discrete species that exist today.

Many will deny that we may have evolved from a primordial wilderness or have any common relationship with other wild creatures. What evidence is there? Let us look at our mountain neighbor, the wolf. It maintains a social order which has leaders and assistant leaders that enforce laws and mete out punishment; courtship between male and female; family groups that work, play, and sing together, provide baby-sitting, and teach; and establish territories with marked boundaries. Wolves will fight and kill intruders. Culture, sex, and violence, it's all there. Sound familiar?

A captive wolf upon release is drawn to and will search out the wilderness environment. It is the Wild Thing calling. The wolf has it and so do we.

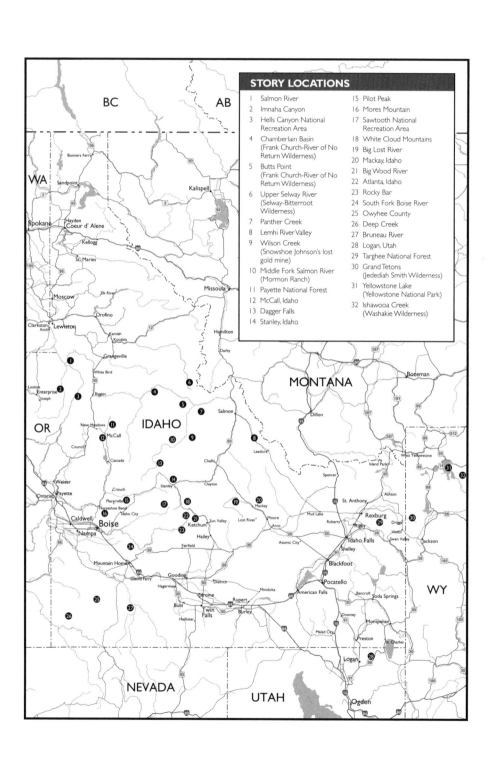

STORY LOCATIONS

1 Salmon River
2 Imnaha Canyon
3 Hells Canyon National Recreation Area
4 Chamberlain Basin (Frank Church-River of No Return Wilderness)
5 Butts Point (Frank Church-River of No Return Wilderness)
6 Upper Selway River (Selway-Bitterroot Wilderness)
7 Panther Creek
8 Lemhi River Valley
9 Wilson Creek (Snowshoe Johnson's lost gold mine)
10 Middle Fork Salmon River (Mormon Ranch)
11 Payette National Forest
12 McCall, Idaho
13 Dagger Falls
14 Stanley, Idaho

15 Pilot Peak
16 Mores Mountain
17 Sawtooth National Recreation Area
18 White Cloud Mountains
19 Big Lost River
20 Mackay, Idaho
21 Big Wood River
22 Atlanta, Idaho
23 Rocky Bar
24 South Fork Boise River
25 Owyhee County
26 Deep Creek
27 Bruneau River
28 Logan, Utah
29 Targhee National Forest
30 Grand Tetons (Jedediah Smith Wilderness)
31 Yellowstone Lake (Yellowstone National Park)
32 Ishawooa Creek (Washakie Wilderness)

1 | The Search

M Y WILDERNESS SEARCH got under way when I was old enough to ride a bicycle, row a boat, and escape on weekends with my pardners, Red Marteness and Bob Jacobs, into the hardwood forests that grew along the Illinois River bottomlands. The best time was early spring when floodwaters would back up into the timber, leaving a few isolated high spots. We would camp on these tiny islands in the woods, listen to the haunting call of the barred owl at night, and pretend we were in the middle of the Okefenokee Swamp. At least the mosquitoes would make you think you were.

In fact, the mosquitoes were so bad we decided to go camping in the winter to avoid them. We saved up our money and purchased what were advertised as "war surplus Arctic down sleeping bags." Years later, when they fell apart, we discovered that the down was actually chopped up chicken feathers. During one Christmas vacation, our parents dropped us off out in the country west of Peoria at the Pottstown Bridge over Kickapoo Creek, which was frozen solid and free of snow. We put on ice skates, shouldered our war surplus rucksacks containing our down sleeping bags and several days' rations of canned pork and beans that froze rock hard by the end of the day, and headed five miles up the creek. By the next morning we were on the fringes of mild hypothermia. We decided we did not wish to carry on this form of recreation for the remainder of the vacation and skated back to Pottstown as quickly as our stiffened bodies would allow. It was another thirty years before I discovered the secrets of winter camping.

The three of us were continually trying to figure out schemes that would allow us to live and make money in the woods someday. Our fur trapping enterprise was a limited success because you could not cover much territory on a bicycle in the morning before school. Unlike most kids today, my bicycle was the only transportation I had until I graduated from high school and earned enough money shucking corn all fall and winter to buy a 1930 Model A Ford.

I had read a magazine article about collecting sap and making maple syrup, which sold at a very high price. The article stated that all species of maple trees could be used but failed to indicate the difference in the sugar content of their sap. The local river bottoms were covered with silver maple, and our fortunes were just waiting to be tapped. We began salvaging large tin cans from the school cafeteria to use as buckets to collect sap from the trees. We cut a six-inch twig, one half inch in diameter, split it in two, and cut a groove down the center for the sap to run in. Then we bored a hole into the tree, hammered in the collector twig, and hung the can off the end. The first drops of sap hitting the bottom of the containers rang like silver dollars coming out of a slot machine.

We were in business and by the end of the week had collected enough sap to make our first run of syrup. We carefully boiled and skimmed sap all day Saturday and continued on the next day until late afternoon when the liquid finally turned into a thin, pale brown syrup. There was about one third of a cup, enough for each of us to get a taste, after which we voted to put the business up for sale.

Other failed ventures included hunting miles of woodlands for ginseng (never found any); picking wild blackberries (we ended up eating them); digging sassafras root to sell in grocery stores as a spring tonic (terminated by a bad case of poison ivy); making wild grape wine (terminated by parents before the juice could ferment).

Do You Prefer Leaded or Unleaded?

Dad always built or owned a boat of some kind, so I was raised on the river, except when I worked on farms during the summer. A fellow upriver, Ben, had a boat landing and floating docks where owners of expensive yachts in Peoria and as far north as Chicago gathered. Several times during the summer, Ben would throw a big party and fish fry at the landing. Dad was one of the best fish cooks on the river, so we always got invited. The landing was also a popular gathering place for the local Huck Finns who had nothing to do, or if they did, found it a good place to hang out. They were mostly my age and our job was to catch bullhead catfish and crappies for the fish fries. This one particular night, it was discovered that the person responsible for the ear corn had failed to deliver. A serious blow to the menu, as fresh corn-on-the-cob was always a feature item.

One of the kids said his uncle had a cornfield a mile down the river that was just getting ripe. Ben would pay four of us to take a boat down to the field and borrow a gunnysack full of corn. He gave us an old, leaking rowboat powered with a 1930 vintage outboard motor. Since the boy's uncle was unaware that we were going to borrow some of his corn and also lived right next to the field, our mission took on the aspects of a night commando raid. We shut off the motor a distance upriver and floated secretly to the levee that separated the cornfield and riverbank.

As we filled a large burlap bag with ears of corn in the darkness, we anticipated the firing of a shotgun and barking hound dogs from the farmhouse. Finally the bag was full and we drug it on a dead run over the levee to the boat and cast off into the river, safe at last, mission accomplished. I wrapped the starter rope around the flywheel, gave it a pull, and the entire back end of the boat and motor went up in flames.

I probably need to describe the level of technology of internal combustion engines that were built in the 1930s. Since there was no fuel pump, gasoline was fed by gravity to the carburetor. Gas flow was controlled by a float and needle valve within the carburetor bowl. It was not uncommon for the float to get stuck in the open position, which allowed all the gasoline in the tank to continue to flow out through the vent at the top of the float bowl unless the main tank valve was turned completely off. This minor detail had been overlooked during the tense moments of our commando raid. The ancient spark plug wires on the outboard motor had become brittle and cracked, and at night you could see electrical sparks arcing through these breaks in the insulation and grounding out on the engine block.

While we were in the cornfield, the carburetor float was stuck in the open position and all the gasoline in the tank drained out over the motor and into the boat. When I pulled the starter rope, I initiated a classic chemical reaction: flammable substance, ignition source, combustion, total chaos. It's amazing how much water four boys can splash with their hands when they really have to. The fire was out, the uncle and his hound dogs were still asleep, there were two more inches of water in the boat, the motor was drowned, and we were a mile downriver and downcurrent from the boat landing.

The one boy suggested getting his uncle to take us back up, but since we had just stolen nearly a hundred pounds of corn from his field, we quickly ruled out that idea and started rowing upstream. By the time we got back to the boat landing, the adults had eaten all the fried fish and were eagerly awaiting the fresh corn. Everyone pitched in shucking corn and putting it in a huge kettle of boiling water that hung over a crackling fire. Soon people were buttering and salting their ears of corn. There was a moment of silent anticipation followed by gagging and kernels of corn hitting the ground like hailstones in a summer storm.

The burlap bag of corn had lain in the bottom of the rowboat for over an hour in a slurry of river water and two-cycle gasoline/oil mixture. This is not a marinade worth passing on except to someone you don't like.

One day we read in the newspaper that Ben had been arrested for shooting a man in his car late one night and dumping the body in the highway. Ben then drove down the road, turned around, and (I guess the guy must have been still wriggling) ran over him on the way back. I'm not sure what business Ben was in or what connections he had, but he claimed self-defense and was never charged. Dad did not go back to the boat landing after that, which was okay with me since I thought he served lousy corn-on-the-cob anyway.

The Money Fish

I spent the year following graduation from high school working full-time on a farm. However, slopping hogs, milking cows, putting up hay, threshing oats, and raising corn was not my career goal. Working in the woods had a lot more appeal until I spent a summer in the river bottoms cutting pulpwood into eight-foot lengths with a double-bit axe and crosscut saw, splitting everything over ten inches diameter with a sledgehammer and steel wedges.

In 1949 I got acquainted with two commercial fishermen, Bill and Beaver Woodruff, who lived up the river north of Peoria near us. Bill taught me how to weave fish nets by hand using a shuttle, mesh gauge, and skein of cotton twine. The basic knot is the sheet bend which has been tied by net fishermen the world over for thousands of years. I learned how to weave hoop (funnel) nets, construct seines, tar nets, and catch carp and buffalo fish, the primary commercial species. The shuttles and mesh gauges I hand carved from Osage orange, an extremely *Shuttle* hard wood native to the south-central states west of the Mississippi. It is the only wood I know of that can withstand the continual abrasion of the twine without wear. The Indians prized Osage for the construction of bows. The tree was unknown to science until 1804, when Meriwether Lewis sent Osage orange cuttings to Thomas Jefferson in the first botanical collection of the expedition.

I also learned from Bill the special technique of trimming out and reweaving holes to properly repair nets. In later years when I was with Idaho Fish and Game, I wrote a publication on net repair illustrating this technique with step by step drawings. It received international distribution, was reprinted in two fisheries textbooks, and was even translated into French for use in the South Sea Islands. I guess I should have hired an agent, because I never made a dime off the publication.

Anyway, old Bill taught me how to make nets, and Beaver taught me how to fish them so the game warden wouldn't catch me. You see, carp and buffalo fish were not what you would call money fish, since they would only bring two and a half cents a pound. You had to catch a lot of fish at that price to make a living. The next problem was that the fish wholesaler was ten miles downriver, might only pay one cent a pound if he was overstocked, or sometimes would not buy any. This meant holding your catches in a live pen until you could market them. I should have researched the business end before tying thousands of sheet bends in miles of cotton twine and building a fishing boat.

Sheet Bend

You may wonder why anyone would want to buy carp in the first place. Rather than go into a great deal of fish history, let me briefly say that the carp has long been a staple diet for millions of people in Asia and was cultivated for the tables of kings in Europe. The carp was so highly prized as a food fish, it was introduced into America in 1877. Carp were released in the Illinois River in 1885 and within thirteen years, produced a commercial catch of 8.3 million pounds. Carp were shipped by rail in wooden barrels filled with ice, arriving live at markets in New York City. The feral carp, unfortunately, did not have the same delicate flavor as those pond-reared in Europe and ultimately received a bad rap. I was raised on carp and have put on carp fish fries at parties and county fairs in Idaho, probably feeding over a couple thousand people with no complaints, only compliments.

But in 1949 there was still a good market for carp. Fillets were retailing at twenty-two cents a pound. I had a few customers who would buy dressed fish from me, but their business was not enough to put gas in the outboard and the Model A; buy licenses, net twine, and tar to preserve nets; and purchase all the other stuff it took to conduct a commercial fishing operation. Beaver Woodruff had the best solution.

At this point in time, the Illinois River was a tremendous natural fish factory. It had not yet been destroyed by pollution from Chicago and topsoil from the central Illinois farmlands. Next to the carp, the most prolific species were the black and the white crappie. These delicious fish were classified by the Illinois Conservation Department as game fish and could not be taken or sold commercially. Consequently, you could bootleg them to customers you knew really well for fifty cents a pound. Crappies were the salvation for the small-time commercial fisherman.

Crappie

Beaver and I would set our hoop nets in the timber during spring flood so that we would be out of sight when we ran our nets. When we caught some crappies, we would put them in a burlap sack along with a couple of bricks. This facilitated rapid sinking of any incriminating evidence as the need arose. The added income from crappie was like getting a federal farm subsidy, and business was looking a whole lot better. I sold the Model A and moved up to a 1935 Hudson Terraplane. I had found my niche and could appreciate how generations of fishermen were drawn to fish and to the sea. You were independent: you built your own boat, weaved your own nets, faced all kinds of weather, and matched your skills with a fish that was often smarter than you.

I always enjoyed being on the river at first light when pulling my string of hoop nets, one reason being that Illinois game wardens never got up that early. I had several hundred pounds of carp in the bottom of the boat and a gunnysack full of crappies. As the sun rose and stretched its rays along the river, I pulled out of the flooded bottomland timber, shut off the motor, and drifted lazily with the slow current.

On the other side of the river was the highway from Peoria to Chicago, but at sunup it was always devoid of traffic. I waved at Beaver as he went by in his flat-bottom boat, headed downriver to pull his nets, hidden like mine in the flooded timber. A pair of male wood ducks in full breeding colors squealed and chased each other in and out of the trees. Somewhere back in the woods, a female perched on a cottonwood limb awaiting the return of her well-dressed suitor. The sun had nudged the red-winged blackbirds from their evening roosts and they were busily establishing territories with their spring song— *konkle reee*. The swollen willow and cottonwood buds were beginning to break open releasing a sweet, pungent sap. I poured a cup of coffee from my thermos, and drank in with it the sounds and smells of the river.

A flock of cormorants landed 100 yards away in the middle of the river and began to get organized for an underwater breakfast foray on schools of gizzard shad. A big, black sedan pulled to a stop on the highway. Four men jumped out and began shooting at the cormorants. I'm sure they were using .45 caliber Colt semi-automatic pistols, as this was the weapon of choice in those days.

The sedan and the cormorants were in direct alignment with my boat. When the first bullet skipped off the water surface and slammed into the trees behind me, I instinctively dove for the bottom of the boat. I was lying there on my stomach in a pile of flopping fish and bilgewater, nose to nose with a big yellow carp, when the shooting stopped and I heard the sedan roaring off to the north. I guess they wanted to get in some target practice before they got to Chicago and started work for the day. I never really felt that I was in any jeopardy after the first bullet sailed in over my head, because I had 200 pounds of fresh carp shielding me from harm's way.

In retrospect, I should have returned the favor and put the carp back in the river, for my commercial fishing days were coming to an end. An unseen cloud, foreboding disaster, loomed on the horizon. Fish biologists were on the river. They conducted a biological survey and concluded that there was an overpopulation of crappies. They recommended classifying the crappie as a commercial fish, thereby increasing harvest, reducing the population, and improving the fishery. Bootleggers—fish or whiskey—don't make much money when their product has been legalized. All of the small-time commercial fishermen went out of business.

I started looking through college catalogs and decided to become one of them fish biologists. I headed for Utah State College in Logan. Without my realizing it, I'm sure Wild Thing had taken control and was pulling me into the mountains.

2 | Out West, Somewhere

D R. WILLIAM SIGLER WAS HEAD of the fisheries school at Utah State and was looking for someone to build and maintain nets for fish collections, and to repair boats. This was a real financial boost over the next four years, since the money from a summer job would not quite get you through the next school year. After all, I was paying $8.00 a month for a two-room log cabin down on the Logan River.

Dr. Sigler had picked up a wooden plank boat from Navy surplus. It was around twenty-five feet long, with an inboard engine and a cabin. He wanted to turn it into a research vessel for Bear Lake. But no one had bothered to check the seams. It leaked so fast when they launched it, the boat sank before they could get it back on the trailer. I had the hull recaulked and painted by the end of spring quarter. When I came back that fall, I was told I did too good of a job. The boat was watertight and floated so high they were fearful it would tip over. This was resolved by pumping water into the boat for ballast. I guess I should have left a few holes in it and saved them all that trouble.

Logan lies within Cache Valley, named for the practice of early trappers caching their furs underground until they could be shipped back to St. Louis. Cache Valley was a favorite wintering area in the 1820s and one of the early locations of the famous trapper rendez-vous. Money could still be made trapping, although the beaver were essentially gone. I ran traplines out in the Bear River marshes and along the Logan River through town. Some of my most productive sets were within the city limits where I picked up domestic mink that escaped from nearby fur farms. My deer meat and money both ran out every year about the time trapping season opened for mink and muskrat in the spring. This would force me into a recycling program. I sold the pelts to the fur dealer to pay for textbooks and I fried up the muskrat carcasses the same as rabbit or squirrel. Some folks will think it disgusting to eat rats, but the muskrat has a pleasant tasting, tender dark meat. At one time, muskrats were served in swank eastern restaurants as a delicacy—under an alias, of course.

Somebody Had to Do It

After my arrival in the Rocky Mountains, I was certain I would never return to Illinois without leaving drag marks all the way back. But I had a job offer one summer that I just could not turn down. It was a job most sport fishermen could only fantasize about: being paid money to fish eight hours a day with a fly rod, given exclusive fishing on thirty-two private ponds for largemouth bass and bluegills, a subsistence allowance, mileage on my car which was now a 1940 Dodge Coupe, and a camp trailer to live in at Lake Glendale in southern Illinois.

The Illinois Natural History Survey was conducting a research project on farm ponds to determine if there was any advantage in fish production and fish size by artificial fertilization of the waters. My assignment was to fish a fertilized pond for half a day and an unfertilized pond the other half—well, somebody had to do it. Records on the catch involved taking length, weight, and scale samples of each fish. The project design also called for removal of all fish caught, so at the end of each work day I was left with a bag full of bass and bluegills. I love to eat fish but after several weeks of three meals of fish a day, I discovered I could trade my day's labor with local farmers for fresh vegetables. By summer's end I had taken over 500 largemouth bass, probably 3,000 bluegills, and could knock a dragonfly off a log with the fly rod and popper bug from thirty feet away.

The only negative part of the southern Illinois job was the chiggers: tiny, red bloodsucking mites that inhabited many of the tallgrass areas. They could migrate up the inside of your pantleg until making contact with skin, then burrow in and make your life miserable. A single chigger could drive a person into an itching frenzy, and I had them on both legs from my ankles to my belt line. A local farmer's wife had given me a homemade remedy she guaranteed would take care of chiggers. I didn't bother to ask what was in it and that night applied it to my body from the waist down. In less than a minute I could almost feel the chiggers struggling to the surface of my skin and leaping off as if to escape a burning building. In less than another minute I knew that I was that burning building and several critical areas were definitely on fire. This was an emergency and no time to stop to get dressed. It was already dark outside, so I ran naked from the trailer out to the end of the boat dock and dove into the lake. Thirty minutes of soaking in the cool water eventually extinguished the flames. The liquid portion of the remedy, I learned, was moonshine whiskey. I think I was supposed to drink it rather than rub it in all over my lower body. But at least all the chiggers had left.

The Real West

The following summer I worked in Yellowstone Park for the U. S. Fish and Wildlife Service (USFWS), primarily collecting and tagging the Yellowstone cutthroat trout. This was 1952 and the USFWS was still operating spawning traps on tributaries of Yellowstone Lake taking cutthroat eggs for shipment to other western states. Although the sport limit was two cutthroat per day, a steady stream of guide boats daily hauled tourists from marinas at West Thumb and Fishing Bridge on the north end, bringing back limits of two-pound cutthroat for everyone on board.

At the same time, fishermen were lined up shoulder to shoulder across the full length of Fishing Bridge, yanking out cutthroat as they moved up the Yellowstone River to spawn. In the frenzy to get their fish out of the river their catch would receive the equivalent of a reverse bungie jump. The trout would go airborne, often landing on the roadway only to get run over by an automobile. In some instances a fish would go through the open window of a passing vehicle.

The fishery was showing signs of decline (I wonder why) so the Park Service enlisted the USFWS to research the problem. Part of the strategy was to capture alive and tag cutthroat to determine migration, exploitation, longevity, and population status. I don't know how long these trout had been trapped, artificially spawned, and the eggs shipped out to other states, but it had gone on for many years. Not only were spawning streams weired off, but at one time lake spawners were collected in a commercial Great Lakes fish trap. The old net had been stored in the loft at the boat house, providing nesting materials for generations of pack rats and mice. The project leader wanted me to put the trap back together and catch trout in the lake to fulfill one of the major objectives of the tagging program. (I always received a certain satisfaction when it took an Illinois carp fisherman to collect fish for a Ph.D.)

There was still a sizeable run of cutthroat up the Yellowstone River that went into the lake. Trout were delayed and congregated where they attempted to move up through the Cascades. I could stand on one particular boulder, make a pass on the downstream side with a large dipnet, and capture five to ten trout on every pass. I was able to tag fifty to one hundred trout daily during the run. One day a special group of entertainers showed up at the head of the rapids. These were Harlequin ducks, now a rare and endangered species. They would dive, feeding on the bottom of the river above the rapids. Then all would ride down through the roaring whitewater like a bunch of crazy kayakers. Time after time they would fly back up-stream for some more snack food and another wild ride.

Research on the cutthroat fishery revealed over-exploitation even with a two-fish daily limit, given the large numbers of fishermen who continually cycled through the park. Ultimately, fishing was re-stricted to catch-and-release, and spawn-taking of cutthroat trout eggs was eliminated.

I spent a two-week tour in an isolated cabin at Grebe Lake help-ing out on a doctorate study there and gill netting fish samples. Grebe Lake had an excellent population of Montana grayling. In fact, the cabin was actually a spawning station for the collection of gray-ling eggs. Seems like if you were a fish living in Yellowstone Park in those days, the government was going to put the squeeze on you. Rainbow-cutthroat hybrids that would nearly rip a fly rod out of your hand after hitting a Renegade dry fly also shared the lake.

Surface residents of interest at Grebe Lake were a family of nest-ing Trumpeter swans and a huge otter. At first, the otter was a nov-elty, but soon became somewhat of a challenge when we went down to the lake in the evening to flyfish. It would spot us fishing and within minutes swim across the lake and sit beside us on the shore like a pet dog, until we hooked a fish. Then it would be in the water like a flash while we ran back up the bank, dragging the fish through the grass with an otter in hot pursuit to see which of us could make the first retrieve and save our dry fly. You then had to sacrifice the fish if you wanted to have at least ten minutes of fishing without run-ning a race with a four-foot otter.

Close Encounters

Everyone at some time in their life experiences one or more close encounters. I've had more than the average, and I often wonder if there are any more holes to punch on my ticket. The first encounter was when I was in diapers and swallowed a button or something that blocked my breathing. A maid at my mother's friend's house grabbed me by the heels and smacked me between the shoulders, dislodging the obstruction. Number Two was when I was ten years old and Dad's boat exploded and burnt to the waterline. I was standing on top of the small cabin, right over the gas tank, when gasoline that had leaked into the bilge ignited, setting the boat aflame from stem to stern. I simply walked across the deck and jumped ashore without singeing a hair. Number Three was being catapulted out of the back of a grain truck that flipped upside down when the tie rod broke. That one cost me some skin and two chipped vertebrae. Number Four was a bit more involved.

Number Four was being stranded in the middle of Yellowstone Lake during a record storm. The boss wanted to make a supply run in the boat down to the Southeast Arm, coming back the same day. The boat was of unknown age, eighteen feet long, with a short cabin and a four-cylinder engine. We had made it about halfway back to the north end, bucking increasing winds and six-foot waves with white-caps crashing over the port bow. I heard something go "kerthunk" and the engine stopped. I tried restarting the engine, but it wouldn't even turn over. Opening the engine hatch, the problem was quickly apparent. I showed the boss the piston connecting rod sticking out of the side of the engine block. He disappeared momentarily and came back out carrying a crescent wrench, screwdriver, and a pair of pliers. Only a Ph.D. in aquatic entomology would have asked you the question, "Can you fix it?"

I think the winds that day were recorded around fifty mph or higher, with a straight blow out of West Thumb for fifteen miles across the lake to our position. Waves were now at least eight feet high. Our drift was taking us into sheer rock cliffs on Pelican Point. With the binoculars I could see the waves hitting the cliffs and shooting spray twenty-five feet up into the air. This did not look like a good place to make a landing.

We had radioed our departure from the Southeast Arm, so we were expected back. The radio, unfortunately, was at the base camp and not in the boat. When we didn't show up in early afternoon, it was obvious we were in trouble and the Park Service was notified. They had a thirty-five-foot, twin engine, cabin patrol boat, and I assumed it would only be a short time before we were located.

Seems the winds were so high and the lake so rough, they decided it was too risky to come out and look for us. Better to wait until evening when maybe the winds would die down. I don't know what the hell they thought they were going to look for by then, except pieces of wood and an oil slick.

An inventory of emergency equipment on board produced a first aid kit, a flare gun, six flares, an anchor, and 100 feet of rope. Setting out an anchor with 100 feet of rope while drifting over 300 feet of water doesn't accomplish much except give you something to do at the moment. I was well aware that with only 100 feet of line, the design of the anchor, the composition of the lake bottom, and the wind velocity we would still drift into the cliff wall where we would then be incorporated into the twenty-five-foot spray.

We were within 500 yards of the cliffs when the anchor grabbed and held. The wind began to abate at sunset and the Park Service nosed its way out onto the lake to search. I saw them approaching and fired off a flare. If I'd known that they had sat on their butts for over six hours while we surfed in eight-foot waves headed for a rock wall, I probably would have fired the rest of the flares into the side of their boat when they came alongside to pick us up.

Another close encounter (though not close enough to be a numbered one) occurred in Yellowstone Park. The Fish and Wildlife Service had a large wooden fish trap that blocked off Pelican Creek as it emptied into Yellowstone Lake. This had to be checked daily during the cutthroat spawning run to count, measure, and tag fish. There had been a large bull moose near the trap, and I planned to bring my camera the next day and take pictures. The following morning, I parked the truck 100 yards back in the timber, walked to the edge of a sand cutbank, and there, twenty feet below, was the bull standing in the middle of the creek. Perfect!

I didn't have a telephoto lens for the camera and wanted a closer shot. The bull seemed unconcerned with my presence, so I slid down the sand bank to the edge of the creek. Who needs a telephoto in Yellowstone Park when the animals stand just fifteen feet away from you? I was adjusting the light aperture on the camera, heard some splashing, and looked up. It was apparent that I was going to get a much closer view of the moose than I really wanted.

If you have ever walked in loose sand, you know how difficult it is, and even more so if you attempt to run, especially uphill. Let me assure you, when you are about to become an ornament dangling from the antlers of a bull moose, a hill of sand is no impediment whatsoever. As I jumped into the truck and slammed the door, the moose trotted past the front of the hood. My next camera would be equipped with a telephoto lens.

I thought Yellowstone would end my search for the ultimate wilderness. Here was territory with unique geologic features and forests that had been protected and preserved, populated with grizzly bear, bison, moose, antelope, elk, and deer. This was the Real West. However, after working in the park, dodging tens of thousands of cars and tourists that swarmed like ants over the trails and through the souvenir shops, and watching people photograph their kids petting black bears that were eating cookies and slices of bread, I felt little remorse when, in September, Wild Thing took me away to continue the search elsewhere.

Deutschland, Danke Onkel Sam

After four years at Utah State, I finally had a piece of paper that said I was a Fish Biologist, but first I had a commitment to take care of. The U. S. Army went to great length and expense to train me as an automotive maintenance specialist, then shipped me overseas in 1954 to Germany as part of the occupation forces. Of course, the Army master plan never intended that I would even come close to an Army vehicle during my tour of duty. Instead, they shipped my personal car, now a 1950 Chevy sedan, across the Atlantic just so I could have something to work on during the next two years.

But a career in the Army ranked somewhat below slopping hogs and milking cows. By June 1956, I had the Chevy running real good, took my discharge papers, bought a brand new Guild guitar with my mustering out pay and headed back west. I must admit though, the Army did introduce me to some new experiences: opportunity to travel Europe, German beer, and my new wife, Maria from Munich.

Utah State University fisheries class collecting carp on the Bear River, May 1953. *Stacy Gebhards photo.*

3 | River of No Return

PRIOR TO MY DISCHARGE, I had corresponded with Jim Simpson, Chief of Fisheries for the Idaho Department of Fish and Game (IDFG), regarding any job openings. He had one on the Salmon River drainage that involved interviewing salmon fishermen for catch statistics, and later in the summer, conducting spawning ground surveys to count spawning beds, depressions that the female salmon digs out in the gravel with her tail to deposit eggs. Our initial base of operations was at Warm Lake in the central Idaho mountains.

Maria wondered what her first home would be like in America. I just said, "trust me." A few weeks later we had set up housekeeping in an eight- by ten-foot wall tent with a sheepherder stove, iron skillet, aluminum cook kit, and two canvas Army cots. Welcome to America! Forty years later, she has fond memories of her first canvas house, but now whenever I use the phrase "trust me," warning flags go up because she knows that something is either wrong or soon will be.

I had never fished for salmon, but was told they could be taken on a red and white spoon. There was a huge log jam in the river near our camp with a deep pool along the edge of it. I cast the spoon to the lower end of the pool and began a slow retrieve. My lightweight spinning rod and six-pound test line were no match for what happened next. I watched a three-foot chinook come out from under the logs, grab my spoon, and swim off downstream stripping all the line off my reel until it came to the end and broke like a thread. In a matter of five seconds, I had hooked and lost the biggest fish I had ever seen.

I returned early the next morning, same rod, same kind of lure, heavier line, same cast, and instantly I had on another big chinook.

This one decided to run upstream and when my line began to reach the end of the reel, I jumped into the river to keep up with the fish. In most places I could run in the shallows and riffles, but occasionally would have to swim through deep pools. At times I felt the fish was playing me on the end of the line and not the other way around. After twenty minutes of running and swimming upriver and back down again, the fish gave out. Here was a fish that had not eaten food for three months, negotiated the dams on the Columbia River, swam upriver 700 miles, and could still fight like a Bengal tiger. I developed such a respect for the chinook that I soon stopped fishing for and killing them, and spent the next thirty-seven years of my professional career dedicated to the protection of this magnificent fish.

The following spring, Maria and I, with newborn daughter Barbara, moved to Salmon, Idaho, at the confluence of the Lemhi and Salmon rivers. The Lewis and Clark expedition first entered the valley through Lemhi Pass in August 1805. Clark made an exploratory trip down the Salmon River to the canyon below North Fork. He found it impassable for canoes and in time it became known as the River of No Return. Trapper journals from 1825 describe the Lemhi Valley as containing hundreds of buffalo. They had long since vanished by 1957, but the Salmon area was still swarming with fish and wildlife. Chinook salmon, steelhead, rainbow trout, pheasants, Gambel quail, grouse, cougar, bobcat, mule deer, and elk could be found within a fifteen minute drive. The city of Salmon still retained the flavor and characters of the Old West, among them Elmer Keith, who developed the .44 magnum. It was not uncommon to see cowboys riding horses into the local bars. When the first drive-in was built, most of the teenagers didn't have cars, so the owners put up a hitching rail so the kids could tie up their horses while they ordered hamburgers and fries.

That fall I shot my first elk, and the next year, Maria killed one of the largest six-point bull elk I have ever packed out of the mountains, though she gives me credit for bugling it into her. By now I had learned the fine art of packing a Decker saddle and shoeing horses. My teacher was Don McPherson, conservation officer at Salmon. He had been raised in the mountains, packed for the Forest Service, and helped his dad, who was a blacksmith. For the next three years, we worked together, fished for salmon, hunted elk, deer, bighorn sheep, and chased cougar and bobcats with his hounds.

Flips and Dips

Dagger Falls on the upper end of the Middle Fork of the Salmon River was thought by some IDFG fisheries experts to be a partial and perhaps serious barrier to migrating salmon. They would point to the obvious fact that fish were concentrated below and could be seen jumping out of the water into the falls. They also ignored the obvious fact that chinook salmon and steelhead had been successfully spawning above the falls in Marsh Creek and Bear Valley Creek for several thousand years.

I became part of a crew sent to collect survey data necessary for an engineering design of a fish ladder around the falls. In 1957, access to Dagger Falls was via a nine-mile horse trail into the Primitive Area from Bear Valley. Conservation officer Phil Swanstrum was to pack in our gear and supplies for a ten-day stay with his string of horses. The civil engineer on the project was a retired World War I Army colonel, now a brigadier general in the reserves. Anyone who has ever been connected with ranking military officers knows that you just do what they ask you, without comment or question. He showed up at the trailhead with his personal gear and bedroll and I do mean **bed**roll. It was a full-size single mattress rolled up in canvas, as big as a Volkswagen sedan. It totally consumed one complete pack horse.

Our project leader was a frugal person. I gave him a list of what I would need in order to take the survey measurements at Dagger Falls, including a sturdy inflatable raft, oars, and lots of heavy manila rope. What I got was a two-man war surplus emergency life raft that was probably left over from the first World War, no oars, and about 300 feet of 3/8-inch rope. At least it was manila.

The engineer, Old Bedroll, needed a series of elevations across the lip of the falls, which, at one place, drops straight down fifteen feet into a plunge pool between two rock walls. No problem. I rigged a double rope anchor line across the river, spliced three lines to the raft with loops on the main anchor line, and had one separate line to hand ferry the raft back and forth. I made a test run and everything worked great.

Close Encounter Number Five was beginning to unfold. I needed an additional person to handle the survey rod while I positioned the raft. With two persons in the raft, the water pressure caused the main anchor line to stretch, forcing us toward the crest of the falls, closer than I wanted to be. As I began to pull back toward the shore, our bargain boat disintegrated.

My passenger washed up on the rock island in the center of the river, out of danger. I was in the main force of the stream with ropes and raft remains draped around me, headed for the big drop. Just above the falls, the river makes a ninety degree turn through a narrow slot, drops about four feet, hits the wall, turns another ninety degrees, and makes the big plunge. I was going through the slot feet first, reached up, and grabbed a rock that projects out over the drop. I wasn't too keen on proceeding any further, so I pulled myself up on the rock and somehow got to the north shore. A forensic specialist could still lift my fingerprints off that rock, even though it's been forty years.

Walt Blackadar was our doctor at Salmon. He had had a similar experience at Dagger, except he had gone over the main drop and nearly drowned. I asked him how deep that plunge pool was. He said he didn't know, but when you were at the bottom, you could not see any light. I was glad I didn't have the opportunity to find out for myself.

The Dagger Falls fish ladder was a controversial project. It was constructed with federal funds without any scientific documentation that fish passage for salmon through the falls was a serious problem. Fish were naturally held up temporarily and congested below the falls, but the greatest obstacle to their passage was an intensive hook and line fishery that took place at the falls. During this period of time, the Middle Fork of the Salmon River was in the Idaho Primitive Area and administrative rules were not as stringent as they are now under the Wilderness Act. The U.S. Forest Service allowed the Idaho Department of Fish and Game to construct a road nine miles into what is now the Frank Church River of No Return Wilderness and a Wild River corridor.

Following completion of the fish ladder in 1959, the Forest Service took over management of the road and built a campground and boat launching facility below Dagger Falls. Prior to this time, all whitewater boating parties had to launch upstream in Marsh Creek or Bear Valley Creek, facing a difficult portage around Dagger Falls before proceeding on down the ninety-five miles of pristine river and rapids. Thus, the fish ladder was instrumental in opening up the Middle Fork to a great influx of commercial and recreational whitewater boating. Once again, a cutthroat trout fishery began to suffer from over exploitation and had to be placed under catch-and-release regulation.

Did the Dagger Falls fish ladder have a positive effect? If you are an outfitter on the Middle Fork or whitewater boater, yes. If you are a cutthroat or bull trout, no. The salmon fishery at the falls was closed, eliminating a sizeable mortality—fish that could now go on to the spawning grounds in Marsh and Bear Valley creeks. In the end, there was no way to statistically demonstrate that the fish ladder significantly enhanced salmon spawning above the falls. Probably closing the hook and line fishing did more.

The River Pilot

As an Illinois farmboy and river-rat, three things amazed me when I arrived Out West: vertical land topography, clear water, and stream bottoms. Vertical mountains I had anticipated, but I had never seen the bottom of a stream in Illinois, let alone drunk from it. I was intrigued by mountain streams and whitewater. Being a riverboat pilot was still a childhood dream and I would study the rapids trying to pick routes and read the waters as Mark Twain might have on the Mississippi.

My first opportunity on whitewater came in 1959. Don McPherson and I were to take the lead raft down the Middle Fork of the Salmon, initiating a research study on cutthroat trout. This would be the first IDFG float trip down the river. Heavy utilization by river outfitters was beginning to cause concern about the status of the cutthroat.

We flew the rafts and supplies into the Indian Creek airstrip. The thirteen-foot rubber rafts were rigged with long paddles, called sweeps, fore and aft, that were set on pivot pins. I had misgivings about the sweeps, but the project leader assured us that he had consulted with a commercial outfitter and this was how the rafts should be rigged. About the third day we pulled in at the Mormon Ranch cabin, owned by Fish and Game, and relaxed in bunks for a change. The next day we planned to float to Wilson Creek, seven miles downstream and camp. The Flying B Dude Ranch is just a short distance below and across the river from the Mormon Ranch. Seemed the neighborly thing to do was to stop briefly and say hello.

I'm a little hazy on the sequence of events that transpired, but six or seven hours later we had lost all our money playing poker and drunk all the beer at the Flying B. Their cook had fallen in love with one of our boat crew and was bawling as we shoved off down the river. So far Don had been operating the rear sweep, but now was in a kneeling position with both arms wrapped around the sweep handle to keep from falling overboard. Our other passenger was face down on the deck, periodically throwing up over the side of the raft.

It seemed like only minutes later we were pulling into the eddy at Wilson Creek after running what we had thought was a relatively flat stretch of river. Actually, this section contains nine Class II and three Class III rapids that require rather precise maneuvering.

We pulled in above Tappan Falls to scout the best route. Don and I had become pretty cocky about our boating skills. Instead of selecting the best route, we went for the best ride, which was right through the center, over a six-foot drop into a hole. Our passenger jumped ship and said he'd walk around and meet us at the bottom, if we made it.

As we started over the drop, I was calmly puffing on a cigar, unaware that my previous misgivings about the raft design had come to pass. The rear sweep had come off the pivot pin and Don was on the deck, hanging on for dear life. With no rear sweep to control it, the raft turned sideways in the hole and I did a backward somersault into the falls. It was like being dropped into a huge bowl of champagne: bubbles everywhere. I knew my life jacket would bring me to the surface, only problem was it jammed me up against the bottom of the raft. I was beginning to wonder if Encounter Number Six was the last space left on my ticket, when the raft hung up momentarily on a rock and I floated out from under it.

The next day we were humbled again at Redside Rapids when the raft broached on the boulder at the bottom of the chute and turned completely over. Lessons learned: tie everything you wish to keep to the boat at all times; don't get overconfident in your abilities; and tuition at the School of Hardknocks can be expensive. In time, skills and raft design improved and I was able to avoid a lot of swimming.

Jolly Green Giant

Government agencies typically lag several years behind the public sector in acquiring the latest technological advancements in equipment. Jet boats were in common usage on the Snake River in Hells Canyon. Since Fish and Game had no way to patrol the river, some people were inclined to ignore hunting and fishing regulations. Eventually, the department allocated money for a jet boat that would operate out of Lewiston. The regional office decided it could save money by designing the boat itself and contracting out the construction.

Jet boats for whitewater are built out of structural aluminum plate. The bow design is flattened and turned upward like a ski tip so the boat will come up out of the water when it hits a wave. The new Fish and Game boat was made of steel plate, overweight, and underpowered.

Bow design was the conventional V-shape, just like an ocean freighter, which I thought was rather appropriate. They painted it green and it became dubbed the Jolly Green Giant.

My job responsibilities as fisheries management supervisor were taking me throughout the state to become familiar with the major waters and their fisheries. Keith Hawn, conservation officer at Lewiston, was captain and pilot of the Jolly Green Giant. Keith had invited me to go with him up Hells Canyon on a trial run and I was looking forward to it with great interest. Jet boat travel on whitewater was going to be an innovation for me, since I was always going one-way through rapids, downstream and not the other way around. The upstream range of the boat was severely restricted, depending upon water flows. Keith wanted to see if he could get up and over Water-spout Rapids in Hells Canyon. Waterspout has a short slick tongue at the top that drops about seven vertical feet. Jolly Green Giant would get part way up and then wash back down. On the third try, Keith backed up for a run at it, hitting the tongue at full throttle. The V-bow split the wave and disappeared. Instantly the entire front end of the boat was underwater and driven to the bottom of the river—kayakers call this an endo maneuver.

The pressure blew out the windshield on my side, a wall of water hit me square in the chest, knocking me to the floor as the canvas roof caved in around me from the water pressure, and Encounter Number Seven appeared to be my final chapter. But for some reason, the boat didn't sink, which, in a way, was too bad, because it was an albatross around the neck of the Lewiston office for a few more years. I was not overly impressed with jet boating and more than ready to return to the old-fashioned way, going with the flow.

Hail to the Chief

It was a week before the President of the United States would be floating the Middle Fork of the Salmon River, and already Secret Service agents were on every sand bar and ridge top, while military helicopters flew up and down the river. Cecil Andrus, then Secretary of the Interior, had invited Jimmy Carter to float the Middle Fork with him and enjoy the Idaho wilderness solitude.

The Forest Service and the Idaho Department of Fish and Game had long desired to get together and have some frank discussions on conflicting policies between the two agencies. What better place to do this than on the Middle Fork, away from phones and distractions, where the cutthroat were sucking in anything that lit on the water's surface and the chukar season was open? The Forest Service was represented by the regional foresters from Missoula and Ogden, forest supervisors from the Salmon and Challis national forests, and the Middle Fork ranger, who operated one of two big Forest Service sweep boats. We had six Fish and Game commissioners, the director, assistant director, and a couple bureau chiefs. Dave Ortmann and I would run two small support rafts.

It required a DC-3 smokejumper plane to fly us and all the gear into Pistol Creek airstrip. I think this may have been the same plane that lost both engines flying into Moose Creek later in the summer and crashed into the Selway River above Wolf Creek Rapids, killing all but one person and a dog.

I was tending the charcoal grill, a two-by-four-foot steel mesh screen on adjustable metal legs. The grill was covered solid with pork chops, liberally coated with barbecue sauce. One of the leaders came over and got down on his knees at one end of the grill. Even on his knees, he was taller than me. He had gotten a jump-start on the cocktail hour and I noticed he was swaying slightly back and forth. His arms at his side, and with no warning, he pitched forward full length onto the pork chops, landing face down with a loud splat.

Being a responsible employee, I grabbed him by the collar and pulled him back to an upright position. He was wearing a brand new, blaze-orange windbreaker, but at this point, looked more like a fresh roadkill. He asked, "Am I hurt?" I answered, "No, Bob, it's only the barbecue sauce." He licked his lips and went off to refill his cup. For some time after that, he was known as Shishka Bob.

Should I turn over yet?

Shish-ka - "Bob"

The campsite at Elk Bar barely had room for us. A platoon from the U. S. Air Force had a tent filled with radio communication equipment that was linked twenty-four hours a day with an Air Force bomber circling overhead, in case the President had to take a phone call. They had spent most of the day repositioning the Forest Service campsite outhouse so that the First Lady couldn't be spied upon if the door wasn't fully closed.

The last day on the river, the commissioners and regional foresters climbed on the sweep boat run by the Middle Fork ranger. I still get nervous thinking about running Redside Rapids on that trip. Just a few years earlier two wooden McKenzie boats had hit a rock at the rapids. Both men—wearing lifejackets—had been thrown into the river and drowned. One body was never recovered.

All the boats made it through the lower river rapids without mishap. There was only one left, Jump-Off Rapids. Dave and I were riding drag behind the main group. As we approached the rapids, I could see in the long pool below the big pontoon raft, but there were no people on it. The paddles on the end of the sweeps were bobbing up and down, four feet out of the water. That didn't make any sense to me until I realized the raft was upside down. Fish and Game commissioners and regional foresters were clinging to rocks along the river's edge.

We picked up what gear was afloat, the ten survivors, and caught up with their raft downstream. At the bottom of the river below Jump-Off lay several thousand dollars in custom imported shot guns, cameras, personal gear, and our lunch. Thinking that nothing could happen to a big raft with thirty-inch tubes, none on board had tied anything down. Makes no difference to the river what the size or design of your craft, they all get the same treatment.

I heard the river ranger that had been at the helm was transferred shortly after that and probably ended his career in some desert outpost in the Southwest where there was no water to deal with. I was not privy to any of the policy discussions between Fish and Game and the Forest Service, since I was usually too busy pulling staff members out of the fire or out of the river. When the news media heard about the flip at Jump-Off Rapids, there was a flurry of concern over the safety of President and Mrs. Carter on their trip down the Middle Fork the following week. From all reports, the Andrus float trip with the President and First Lady was uneventful. They should have gone down with us.

The author with 4,000 trout in a plastic bag filled with three quarts of water and inflated with pure oxygen. *Walt Bethke photo; courtesy Idaho Department of Fish and Game.*

4 | High Mountain Trout

Four-legged Fish Trucks

OVER THE PAST THREE MILLION YEARS, Idaho has intermittently been buried under glaciers, some up to a mile thick. Mountain peaks such as Borah, Heyburn, and Trinity were simply tiny rock islands in a sea of ice. The last Ice Age terminated only 10,000 years ago and the scars left by those rivers of ice are today's valleys and lakes. There are around 2,000 alpine lakes in Idaho which are breathtaking in their beauty and their trout fishing, but how did those fish get there? Only a few lakes had a stream access that fish could negotiate, gain entry to the lake, and establish a population.

Starting in 1920, the Fish and Game Department and Forest Service began hauling trout in ten-gallon milk cans on pack mules and horses into the backcountry lakes of the Sawtooth Mountains. Ice was added to keep the water cool, and one pound of one-inch trout could be kept alive for several hours. With a milk can on each side, a mule had a 220 pound pack. The fish often did not make it to the lake, either because they ran out of oxygen, the water warmed too much for the trout, or they became victims of a mountain rodeo that dumped the cans and fish into the rocks.

Not much changed in the design of this transportation system, except canvas bags were substituted for the cans. In 1960, I began experimenting in using three-gallon plastic bags inflated with pure oxygen as fish containers. Eighteen ounces of fish, up to 4,000 small trout, could be carried in three quarts of water—enough fish to stock an entire lake. This unit weighed seven pounds compared to ninety-five pounds with the canvas bags. Two bags fit inside a packbox lined with one-inch sheets of Styrofoam. A couple scoops of crushed ice over the bags kept the water temperature below forty-five degrees for twelve hours. We rarely lost a single fish in transit.

I could load three boxes on a single pack animal, enough bags and fish to stock six lakes—the old way would have taken three pack animals. I was pleased that I had improved fish survival and the efficiency of mountain lake stocking, reducing program costs by two-thirds. In the process, I pissed off every conservation officer in the state that owned horses. The only way most of them could afford to keep horses was with the rental money they received from the department for packing fish in the summer.

Bombs Away

One of the earliest unconfirmed attempts at aerial fish stocking may have been in north Idaho in 1919. The first recorded experiments on aerial drops and fish survival were in 1938 by Lionel Dean of Twin Falls, Idaho. He began working on a fish tank that would fit in the passenger seat of an open cockpit Eaglerock biplane. In July, 1941, 80,000 fingerling trout were stocked from the air in thirty-eight lakes of the Sawtooth Mountains.

In central Idaho, a common technique was to carry fish in milk cans in a Ford Tri-Motor and pour the contents out the open door of the plane. My guess is that the person with the least seniority got to do the pouring. A more sophisticated system was developed in 1949. This was a double compartment tank holding thirty gallons of water that was aerated by an airscoop. Each flight was limited to stocking of only two lakes.

The plastic bags were a natural for hauling fish in small planes. All I needed was a device for releasing the fish. I took a milk strainer, which is basically a large funnel, fit it with a rubber stopper at the bottom, then attached an aluminum pipe that went through the floor of the plane to the outside. A backcountry pilot, Larry Johnson of Hailey, had a stagger-wing D-19 Beechcraft biplane that he was willing to use and allow us to cut a hole in the floor.

We loaded up thirty bags, each labeled with the name of the lake. On the approach I would cut open the bag and pour the fish and water into the funnel. Larry would yell when we were over the lake, I'd pull the plug, and the fish were sucked out and airborne. Forward trajectory of the fish was short, then they fell straight down. Air resistance prevented lethal velocities on impact with the water surface, so we could safely drop them from 500 feet or more without visible mortality as long as they didn't land in the trees. Numerous observations at lakes following an aerial drop were made on the surface and with scuba gear. No dead or dying fish were ever found.

One day we stocked a number of lakes in Copper Basin and the upper Big Wood River. Flying into these restricted lake basins is best done at first light when the air is stable, cool, and dense. For some reason we decided to push it and finish off with a flight into some lakes in the Sawtooth Mountains later in the morning. As the sun hits the granite cliffs and warms the air, mountain flying becomes unpredictable. I was fully aware of this, so when Walt Bethke, superintendent of the Mackay Fish Hatchery, and Sam McNeill, conservation officer at Stanley, expressed interest in taking the next flight, I relinquished my seat without hesitation.

It had been a rough flight and they were making the approach on the final lake. Walt had the fish in the funnel waiting for the signal to release. Sam was up front with the pilot, acting as spotter and navigator. Walt heard a yell, pulled the plug, and looked back out the window to see if the fish hit the lake. Only there was no lake, just lodge-

pole pine, spruce trees, and rocks below. The signal Walt heard had been Sam puking his breakfast into the instrument panel.

By 1964, we added helicopters to the plastic bag transport and mountain lake fish stocking was almost totally converted to aerial drops. Now the conservation officers were really pissed at me. My son, John, working at the McCall Fish Hatchery in 1984, invited me to go along on a fish stocking flight. Here was John using the same techniques I had put together before he was born. Bill Dorris of McCall Air Taxi was our pilot and flying conditions were perfect. We dropped fish in lakes on the headwaters of the South Fork of the Payette River, Queens River, and along the crest of the Sawtooths. The last lake was on Alpine Creek, elevation 8,700 feet. Approach is always from above, cutting the power to drop in on the lake, release the fish, and then full power out. As the pilot banks the plane, you can look back and see the fish hitting the surface of the lake like a string of raindrops for about 100 feet or so.

On this particular lake we released a few seconds late. As I looked back I could see fish hitting the water right up to the edge of the lake and on into the doorway of a backpacker tent. I could imagine this person spending at least two days hiking into the wilderness. Then lying in his sleeping bag at the edge of this pristine lake, waiting for the first rays of sunlight, he is suddenly bombarded with wet fish from a roaring airplane. I thought for sure Fish and Game would get an obscene letter, but I guess he didn't know who to send it to.

Bottom Fishing and Body Piercing

Walt Bethke and I hunted and fished a lot together when he was still assigned at Mackay Hatchery. I think our favorite quarry was whitefish in the winter on the Big Lost River. There was one special hole we had taken a lot of fish from. We were curious how many whitefish could be left as the season was coming to an end on the first of February. I said, "Walt, there's one sure way to find out—join 'em."

I was lying on my stomach, six feet underwater, on the bottom of the Big Lost River with a two-foot fishing rod in my hand and wearing forty pounds of lead on a weight belt so I would not drift through with the current. Several feet downstream, a dozen whitefish lined up side by side, with apparent curiosity, as I pulled some line off the reel. I was using my kids' toy pole and reel. I moved the baited hook slowly in front of the largest whitefish, and he slurped it in.

Up on top, Walt was sitting on a snowbank in a blinding snow-storm, wondering if it took a college degree to do something this stupid. A black form in a rubber suit, face mask, and scuba tank surfaced like a whale, playing a whitefish on the end of a toy rod and reel. It had taken only twenty-two seconds to dive down, locate, and hook the fish. With numbing fingers, Walt removed the fish, rebaited my hook with a stonefly nymph, and I again disappeared beneath the surface of the water and the snowstorm. I was catching two fish per minute and having a blast in the thirty-six degree water. At this rate, I could limit out in twenty-five minutes, but by fish number six, it was evident that Walt would not last that long. The storm had gotten worse and so had he. As he headed for the truck, he said that if I wanted to lay on the bottom of the river and fish just so I could get out of the storm, I could find someone else to bait my hook.

As far as I know, it is legal to fish underwater, I mean literally. You don't waste time, as you often do on the surface, casting where there are no fish. You select the very fish you want. It doesn't matter what the weather is doing. Your line doesn't freeze in the guides when you are winter fishing. I can't understand why more fishermen haven't picked up on this technique.

Walt and I also fished in the more conventional manner, during the summer, out of a boat on Mackay Reservoir. Around 1960 the reservoir produced some lunker rainbow trout. We fished for these with spinning rods and a heavy, three-inch red and white striped spoon called a Daredevil. On the terminal end of the spoon was a large treble hook. Three of us were in a small boat with Walt sitting on the middle seat. The fellow at the front of the boat, in his haste to get the first lure in the water, failed to pay attention to the location of his rod tip and hook as he made a strong forward cast.

Walt let out a yelp and I turned around to see a red and white fishing lure dangling from his right cheekbone. The hook had gone through the skin and back out again. We didn't have any tools that would cut through the shank of the hook or bend down the barb, so we headed for town. Mackay, Idaho, wasn't much of a town and it had the medical services to match. When I suggested going to the doctor there, Walt said he'd rather wear the fishing lure permanently.

I knew Lon Jarvis, who ran the hardware store in Mackay, and told Walt to wait in the truck while I went into the store. I asked Lon if he had a good pair of sidecutters I could borrow for a minute. In the meantime, Walt had gotten out and was leaning on the truck visiting with a group of onlookers. This was long before body-piercing had become a fad and it was an unusual sight for Lost River cowboys and ranchers to see a grown man with trinkets attached to parts of his face. A quick snip with the sidecutters and the hook was removed amid a round of applause from the sidewalk spectators.

Frying the State Record Trout for Breakfast

All four of my kids have shared with me a passion for the mountains and fishing the backcountry lakes. We had backpacked into the Sawtooths to do some early fall fishing in September 1976, prior to the start of school. Many lakes in the 1920s were initially stocked with eastern brook trout. This proved to be a poor choice. Brook trout are prolific spawners and soon overpopulate a lake, becoming thin and stunted. Attempts to reduce brook trout numbers by increasing bag limits and stocking other trout species as predators have not been successful, and the lakes end up with a mix of trout species.

We were hooking a few six-inch brookies when Barb landed a fourteen-inch trout. She asked, "Dad, what kind of a fish is this? It looks different." What better authority could she go to but the then chief of fisheries for the entire state of Idaho. It looked like a cross between a brook trout and a Dolly Varden. I knew that Dollies had been stocked in some lakes as potential predator fish. I told her it was probably a hybrid, as both species are fall spawners.

Next morning I filleted the fish and was so struck by the vivid red coloration of the flesh that I took a color photo of it before dropping it into the skillet. On the trip home, I had a nagging recollection of an old report on file from the 1920s that recorded stocking of Sunapee trout in the lake we were fishing. The Sunapee is a char, originally found only in Sunapee Lake in New Hampshire. I found a book that had color photos of the Sunapee and there it was. Barb's fish was the first Sunapee trout ever known to be taken in Idaho. Technically, she had caught the state record, since this species had never before been listed, but the chief of fisheries had fried and eaten it for breakfast.

5 | Encounters Number Eight and Nine

MOUNTAIN STATES, LIKE IDAHO, rely heavily on small aircraft and helicopters for transportation of supplies, equipment, mail, and people. Flying is almost a way of life for an Idaho Fish and Game employee. We conduct fish surveys, big game surveys, waterfowl surveys, stock fish, capture and relocate bighorn sheep and mountain goats, herd animals, track radioed animals, and make enforcement patrols with helicopter or fixed-wing aircraft. The workhorse in the backcountry is the single-engine Cessna 206 which can carry the pilot and five passengers or a payload of 1,000 pounds adjusted to altitude, air temperatures, and condition of the airstrip.

Once a regional personnel meeting scheduled in Lewiston required the attendance of the headquarters staff. A local flying service was to take five of us, leaving Boise at 6:00 a.m. Passengers were the Fish and Game director, assistant director, two bureau chiefs, and me. The sky was overcast as a weather front was moving in and the ceiling was dropping.

We had passed over the ridge into the head of the Imnaha River as the clouds began to close in around us. Just then the rpm's dropped and the engine sounded like the cylinders were full of marbles. The decrease in power caused the tail to drop. I was in the rear seat and was now about two feet lower than the pilot. It had begun to rain and visibility was only a few hundred yards, enough to make out the rock cliffs on either side of us as we sputtered down the Imnaha Canyon. I felt a little better as we entered the Snake River. If we had to, we could land on water, which is a lot softer than rock. For an entire hour the pilot had not said a word as he chain-smoked one cigarette after another. But we did make it to Lewiston. A fellow from the regional office picked us up at the airport. All he had to say about our experience was, "Glad you guys made it okay, but it sure would have opened a lot of promotional opportunities." When the plane's engine was examined, part of the camshaft had broken and the plane had lost function in two cylinders. We returned to Boise on a commercial airline.

Don't worry,
I've got another
pack of cigarettes.

The next spring, after another meeting in Lewiston, the director and I flew back to Boise in a Cessna 206 and a state aeronautics pilot—I refused to fly anymore with a certain local flying service. Thunderstorms were moving through, side by side. The pilot decided he could go underneath the weather by taking a low elevation route and following the Snake River up through Hells Canyon. This worked until we came around a sharp turn in the canyon and were engulfed in a wall of rain, zero visibility, and violent turbulence. I now know how a dirty sock must feel in the wash cycle of a washing machine.

Then, just as suddenly, we were back out of it and headed downstream. The pilot had been able to negotiate a 180 degree turn without slamming into the side of the canyon. So far, so good, I thought. We'll go back to Lewiston and wait for better weather. As we came back around the same turn again, a half-mile downstream we confronted another solid wall of water clear across the canyon. We were trapped between two severe thundershowers and not much room to mess around in with an airplane. The pilot was new to Idaho, unfamiliar with the canyon. He suggested we try to get out over the Seven Devils mountains. I told him I didn't think that would be a good alternative under these conditions and in case he didn't know where we were, the emergency air strip at Oxbow Dam was right below us. We landed there and waited out the storm. They say timing is everything.

My daughter, Sandy, has an appreciation for timing as it relates to backcountry flying as well. She was managing the old Stonebraker Ranch in Chamberlain Basin, within the Frank Church River of No Return Wilderness. Ground access was some twenty-five miles of trail through the mountains, but there was also a good dirt airstrip nearby. Guests and hunters that stayed at the ranch were usually flown in, along with all the supplies. Sandy had made a trip out to town and hooked a ride back in to the ranch on the mail plane—once a week, Ray Arnold, who operates a flying service out of Cascade, delivered mail, groceries, equipment, and passengers to the various outposts scattered about the Salmon River wilderness. They made a stop at the Flying B Ranch on the Middle Fork of the Salmon, then took off for Chamberlain Basin. As they began to climb out of the river canyon and head for the high country, two cylinders cracked on the engine of the 206, spraying oil over the windshield. Ray had just enough power to negotiate a tight turn within the river corridor and make it back fifteen miles to the Flying B for an emergency landing. Had the engine problem developed five minutes later into the flight, the engine would have seized up and dropped them into the side of a mountain.

Ray also often transports cats to the backcountry ranches to provide some added company, and, more importantly, to serve as the primary means of mouse and gopher control on the ranch. During one of his feline deliveries, the cat got out of its container box and became very upset that it was confined in a noisy, vibrating airplane. It began doing 360s around the inside of the cockpit and on Ray's head, which was bound to be a distraction when trying to land on a difficult backcountry airstrip. At the time, Ray was about halfway across the Frank Church Wilderness, flying at 10,000 feet. The third time the cat came across the instrument panel, Ray opened the side window and the cat jumped out. This was a rare example of good and bad timing occurring simultaneously. I have often wondered what would have happened if the cat landed in the middle of a string of pack mules. I also wonder if it lit on its feet.

East Fork Owyhee River, May 1983. *Stacy Gebhards photo; courtesy Idaho Department of Fish and Game.*

Sawtooth Lake and Mt. Regan, Sawtooth National Recreation Area. *Stacy Gebhards photo.*

The author's family in Idaho's outdoors. *Opposite above:* Barb and John, Sawtooth National Recreation Area, 1976. *Opposite below:* Sandy in the Mountain Home desert. *Top:* Maria above Roaring River, Boise National Forest. *Bottom:* Judi and John, East Fork Salmon River, Sawtooth National Recreation Area, March 1980. *All photos by Stacy Gebhards.*

Above: Walt Bethke at Moose Lake, Big Lost River. *Stacy Gebhards photo; courtesy Idaho Department of Fish and Game. Opposite above:* Floyd Harvey, Arthur Godfrey, Burl Ives and Walter Hickel at Willow Creek Camp, Hells Canyon on the Snake River, May 1970. *Stacy Gebhards photo; courtesy Idaho Department of Fish and Game. Opposite below:* The author finishing a diamond hitch, East Fork Moose Creek, Selway/Bitterroot Wilderness. *Wes Rose photo.*

Opposite above: Upper Queens River and Mt. Everly, July 1985. *D. Cadwallader photo; courtesy Idaho Department of Fish and Game. Opposite below:* Hells Canyon. *Stacy Gebhards photo; courtesy Idaho Department of Fish and Game. Above:* John Gebhards in a telemark turn, Freeman Peak, Boise National Forest, February 1981. *Stacy Gebhards photo.*

A conservation officer in "Kayak School" on the South Fork Payette River, June 1981. *Stacy Gebhards photo; courtesy Idaho Department of Fish and Game.*

6 | Blue Lights on Whitewater

THE FISHERMAN HAD GONE TO A LOT OF EFFORT, crawling through thorn-covered wild rose, poison ivy, and dense brush to get to the river's edge. Now he could relax, completely hidden from view, and start fishing in the Boise River without a fishing license. Upstream, an Idaho Fish and Game officer was quietly drifting along in his kayak when he saw the tip of a fishing rod emerge from the willows and a baited hook plop into the water. A draw stroke pulled the kayak into the bank. The officer peered up the pole to find a startled fisherman at the other end. You can guess what his first comment was upon seeing the Fish and Game badge on the officer's life jacket. His second comment was, "I don't believe it, this can't be happening to me."

One spring day, we were kayaking on the South Fork of the Boise below Anderson Ranch Dam. Fishing season was still closed to protect spawning rainbow trout. I came around a bend on a remote section of the river, and there was a fisherman standing on a large rock out in the river. He was so intent on snagging a big spawner with a treble hook he did not realize anyone was within miles of him, until a kayak eddied out below his rock at the toes of his boots. His surprise quickly turned to rage at having my kayak plugging up his fishing hole. He was on the verge of sticking his foot through the deck of my fiberglass kayak when I informed him I was a Fish and Game officer and fishing season was closed. It's too bad no track and field officials were present, because this guy no doubt set a world record in the standing long jump and 400 meter dash in hip boots.

Enforcement of fishing regulations on 16,000 miles of Idaho streams is unique and difficult. Most are mountain streams, often accessible only by floating, or hiking on primitive trails. Over 1,000 miles have special restrictive regulations necessary to protect and enhance wilderness species like the Westslope cutthroat, redband trout, bull trout, salmon, and steelhead. Traditional methods of patrol by vehicle at access points, foot, horseback, rafts, and powerboats, left yawning gaps in the coverage of 16,000 miles of waters. The Middle Fork of the Salmon and Selway Rivers, which had 200 miles of stream requiring catch-and-release of all fish, are in the national Wild River classification that restricts motors. Even on rivers patrolled by outboard and jet boats, illegal fishermen clean up their act as soon as they hear an engine approaching.

In 1980, I reviewed these enforcement problems with the Fish and Game Commission and proposed the training of conservation officers for kayak patrols. This would greatly expand their range of effectiveness. Kayaking was a fast-growing recreational sport in Idaho. If the public knew that Fish and Game officers also kayaked, it could be a real deterrent. The Commission approved the purchase of kayaks and authorized the training of personnel.

I put together an intensive five-day training program and enlisted my son John, who at fifteen was already an expert kayaker, as an assistant instructor. Most of the twelve recruits who volunteered that first year had never seen a kayak up close, and they had little experience in whitewater boating. Several of the conservation officers were essentially cowboys and much more at home in the saddle on top of a horse. This was quite evident the first few days on the river as these individuals habitually reached for a saddle horn when they started to tip over.

By the end of the fifth day, they had forty hours of kayaking, starting with the basics and working up until they were punching Class III rapids like a bunch of Harlequin ducks. Their graduate course was a run down the Middle Fork of the Salmon.

Kayak patrols produced some interesting encounters. One officer, distracted by a sunbather, was unaware that he was being swept into a low hanging tree until the limbs started banging into his helmet. He escaped amid broken limbs, leaves, and some desperate paddling. His excuse was that he was trying to see if she had a fishing pole, which was unlikely since women lying on their backs in bikinis usually are not fishing, at least for fish. On another occasion, an officer came upon a young lady fishing topless, but was too embarrassed to stop and ask to see her license. A more fearless officer ran the same section of river the following day and issued her a citation. You can fish topless in Idaho, but not without a fishing license.

In three years, some thirty personnel were trained and Idaho was credited as being the first state to have officers qualified in whitewater patrol with kayaks.

Thread-the-Needle Rapids, East Fork Owyhee River, May 1983. *Stacy Gebhards photo; courtesy Idaho Department of Fish and Game.*

The author operating his "dishwasher" at Stonebraker Ranch, Chamberlain Basin. *Beth Workman photo.*

7 | The Sound of Music and Politicians

THE IDAHO WILDLIFE FEDERATION was planning its annual winter meeting and asked if I could provide some musical entertainment at the banquet. Environmental awareness was just beginning to gain national attention and they wanted something along that theme. I enlisted the help of two folk singers who also played guitars, Nancy Oakes and Anne James from Boise.

Our feature song was a parody I wrote from the old western song "Cool Water." The first chorus was original lyrics, then came the parody, listing Idaho streams and their polluted conditions. All this was sung while showing color slides on a large screen of crystal clear streams followed by the bad and the ugly. The pollution slides were quite graphic, showing actual photos of the streams mentioned in the song. The response we received was tremendous.

About a month later I got another call from the Federation. Floyd Harvey, an outfitter at Lewiston, had been successful in organizing a jet boat trip into Hells Canyon for Burl Ives, Arthur Godfrey, and Walter Hickel. The purpose of this trip was to generate interest and national publicity for the support of congressional legislation to establish the Snake River in Hells Canyon as a protected national river and exclude dam construction. Several federal proposals for high dams in Hells Canyon were in the active planning stages and being endorsed by the governor of Idaho.

Burl Ives was known the world over as a ballad singer and movie star. His first song book also diagrammed guitar chords for each song. I bought the book and a $25 Stella guitar in 1948. Arthur Godfrey made movies, but was more famous for his national radio program. Walter Hickel, former governor of Alaska, was the Secretary of the Interior. The Federation was holding a banquet in Lewiston on May 22, 1970, the evening before the jet boat trip upriver, and they asked Nancy, Anne, and me to put on our show again.

My contact wanted to know if we could write a song about Hells Canyon. I wrote lyrics to "Wild River" and Anne put it to music. I also did a story song about a chinook salmon that travels up the rivers to Idaho. It was entitled "Dammit." Rosalie Sorrels, Idaho's premier folksinger, had written a song called "White Clouds" that painted the beauty of this mountain range and the devastation that would come to it with a proposed open pit mine. She gave us permission to use her song at the banquet. Now, in addition to "Cool Water," I had assembled slide programs to accompany "Wild River," "Dammit," and "White Clouds." As if playing a five-string banjo wasn't enough of a challenge, I sang harmony while changing slides on the projector with a foot switch.

Governor Don Samuelson was up for re-election in the fall. He had insisted that Idaho was a clean water state, therefore pollution control was a non-issue. The governor endorsed high dams in Hells Canyon that would destroy Idaho's salmon and steelhead runs and flood the deepest whitewater gorge on earth. He strongly favored a proposal to allow open-pit mining at the base of one of Idaho's most spectacular mountain gems, Castle Peak. It was no surprise that Governor Samuelson was not invited to the Lewiston banquet.

But he crashed the gate anyway and sat down next to Secretary of the Interior Hickel at the head table. The Department of Interior at that time administered and enforced federal water quality standards in the United States—this was prior to establishment of the Environmental Protection Agency. The governor, I can imagine, was espousing his clean water programs to the secretary as the house lights dimmed and we kicked off with our first number, "Cool Water." When the show was over and the lights came back on, Samuelson was already on his way out the door.

I spent the next two days at Floyd Harvey's Willow Creek Camp with the boat tour and even cooked carp for them as hors d'oeuvres. I was especially honored to loan my guitar to Burl Ives for the campfire songs in the evening.

When I got back to Boise, Dick Woodworth, Fish and Game director, called me into his office. He suggested it might be a good idea, if we all wanted to keep on working for Fish and Game, to hang up my banjo and stop singing songs for a while. The governor had flown back to Boise right after the banquet, called the chairman of the Fish and Game Commission in the middle of the night, and informed him that if I did another show, he would have a new Commission and director appointed the following day. I probably wouldn't be too far behind those who were leaving.

The governor knew who I was and had assumed the programs were Fish and Game productions. What he didn't know was we had done everything on our own time and expense. We were scheduled to do the show the next weekend for the annual meeting of the Idaho League of Women Voters. I called the program chairwoman and said we had to cancel out. She asked why, and I told her. Within ten minutes, I had calls from the Associated Press and UPI wanting to know what was going on between the governor of Idaho, a state employee, and freedom of speech. The governor had naturally been embarrassed before the Secretary of Interior and thought it inappropriate that I showed dirty pictures of Idaho streams. When the press interviewed him, his comment was, "If he isn't any prouder of our state than he indicates, then he should move on." The governor maintained that the photos depicted conditions that existed twenty-five years ago and not at present. Of course, the press immediately followed up on his accusation. The color slides were all dated with the month and year of processing: 50 percent of them had been taken in 1970 and the oldest photo was dated 1966.

During this same time period, I had produced a twenty-minute 16mm movie film for Fish and Game entitled *The Vanishing Stream.* It summarized the results of a two-year research project we had done on the extent and impacts of stream channel alteration on fisheries in Idaho. The movie also portrayed loss of streams through dam construction and pollution from all sources. The governor didn't like the movie any better than my singing. Our objective was to arouse public awareness and support for a legislative Stream Protection Act.

The governor took a beating from all over the state in editorials, cartoon pages, and letters-to-the-editor. Election day came and went and so did Don Samuelson. Cecil Andrus, who had supported our efforts, songs, and stream protection legislation was elected governor. Andrus went on to serve as Secretary of Interior during the Carter Administration, and was reelected governor upon his return to Idaho. Had the election turned out differently, I probably would be back on the Illinois River trying to seine carp and bootleg crappies for a living.

Wild River

In the mountains of the Yellowstone
Was born a tiny stream
Whose beauty and attraction
No one would ever dream.

In the shadows of the Tetons
Her fingers weave and toil,
From rocky cliffs to gentle slopes
She shapes the land and soil.

Her children follow in her path,
Big Wood and Thousand Springs.
The Bruneau and the Buffalo,
Their music softly sings.

A man has come and stolen her charms,
And scarred her lovely face.
He uses her to do his work,
She fights to leave this place.

A kinder man awaits her here.
She's home now, safe, secure.
Seven Devils are guarding her,
Her spirit's free and pure.

She travels wide and rambles far
And then no more will roam.
Wild River, Wild River,
Hell's Canyon will be your home.
—Stacy Gebhards

Dammit

A chinook was swimming in the Bering Sea when a cute little chick
   swam by.
She said "Honey, follow me to Idaho, have some fun before you
   die."
"I'd have to swim 4,000 miles, answer me this question, why,
Why the hell should I do all that if I'm just gonna spawn and die?"

He followed her to the Columbia, through gill nets and treble
   hooks.
Said, "Baby, I wouldn't follow you, if it weren't for your good looks."

"Dammit" he said as a shark swam by, "answer me this question, why,
Why the hell am I doing this, if I'm just gonna spawn and die?"

Astoria, Oregon, a fearsome place, past here they quickly ran.
She said, "Honey, don't let them take you there, you can't make love in a can."
"Dammit" he said as he fought the nets, "answer me this question, why,
Why the hell am I doing this, if I'm just gonna spawn and die?"

"Dammit" he said, and dam it they did, as he crashed into a wall.
An ugly chunk of concrete, named Bonneville, first of all.
"Dammit" he said, "and there's seven more, answer me this question, why,
Why the hell am I doing this, if I'm just gonna spawn and die?"

His nose was bent and his hide peeled off, "A ladder is what I'll need."
The Corps of Engineers said, "Jump again, all you need is a little more speed."
"Dammit" he said as he rammed a barge, "answer me this question, why,
Why the hell am I doing this, if I'm just gonna spawn and die?"

Nitrogen gas and diesel oil and beer cans floated by.
As he entered the Snake, he began to shake, and tears were in his eye.
"Dammit" he said as he coughed and bled, "answer me this question, why,
Why in the hell am I doing this, if I'm just gonna spawn and die?"

Riggins and Challis and Sunbeam Dam, and Stanley town they passed.
They ran out of water at Decker Flats and knew they were home at last.
"Dammit" he said as he dodged a spear, "answer me this question, why,
Why in the hell did I do all this, if I'm just gonna spawn and die?"

Four thousand miles of misery, three months gone without food.
"I've taken all I'm gonna take, I hope you're in the mood."
"Dammit" he said, "I cannot wait, my time has come," he cried.
She winked her eye and wriggled her tail, and he spawned right there and died.

—Stacy Gebhards

Music by Maytag

Other instruments I learned to play were a chromatic harmonica and a two-row button accordion, or diatonic accordion. I learned the squeeze box from my old friend, Joe Kozlowski, at Logan, Utah, in 1952. I built a strong plywood carrying case for it, to withstand bucking pack horses, river rafting, and even backcountry ski trips. When someone sees the beat-up box for the first time, they ask me what's in it. I tell them, "That's my dishwasher." The way it works is to pull the accordion out and start playing it right after dinner. Someone will always say, "You keep right on playing, we'll do the dishes." I haven't had to do dishes in camp for going on forty-five years. What I should do is paint over the manufacturer's name, Hohner, and put on Maytag.

During the summer of 1963, we were on a field inspection trip in the upper South Fork of the Boise River with the Forest Service. The federal government owned and managed over 60 percent of the state of Idaho, and annual show-me trips were standard occurrences. By the second night in camp, the beer was gone and the nearest filling station was the bar at Paradise Hot Springs below Featherville. A bunch of us piled into a carryall and headed the fifteen miles downriver. The bar was filled with local gold miners, loggers, and Air Force personnel from Mountain Home Air Base.

Over in a corner was an old miner, Three-Fingers Duncan, who had received a two-row button accordion by mail-order. He was having trouble trying to get any music out of it. One of our group knew him, asked to borrow it for a bit, and handed it to me. The first tune I cranked out was "Lili Marlene." This was the number one song in Germany during WW II. A lady at the far end of the room from Heidelberg jumped up on the bar and started singing.

For the next three hours I played non-stop. Everyone kept buying beers for the accordion player, but wouldn't let me stop playing long enough to drink any of them. Soon my end of the bar was covered with beer cans. My buddies from camp volunteered to help me out so I could keep on playing. Around 1:00 a.m. the bar closed, I gave Three-Fingers back his accordion, pushed aside a pile of empty beer cans, loaded a bunch of drunks into the carryall, and drove them back to camp.

I was invited on a four-day raft trip through Hells Canyon in May 1971, sponsored by the Hells Canyon Preservation Council, and told to bring my dishwasher, harmonica, and guitar. The group included

Oregon Senator Bob Packwood, Jack Hemingway, and Dr. Walt Blackadar bobbing alongside in a kayak. Blackadar had gained a national reputation as a kayaker, having pioneered first descents on rivers that had been classed as unrunnable by most whitewater experts. Packwood was the moving force in the U. S. Senate to get a national rivers bill passed to preserve the Snake River in Hells Canyon.

The trip consisted of a bunch of people, wives included, and required two thirty-foot rubber pontoon rafts. Each raft carried fifteen people, plus food and gear. The Snake River was at flood stage, the highest I had ever seen it. The rafts had plywood decks, fore and aft, that were outfitted with a set of long oars and oar locks. I was selected to run the forward set of oars on our raft. Vern Huser, river guide and outdoor book author, manned the rear. Wild Sheep Rapids at this water level was more than awesome. At the head of the rapids was a huge, breaking diagonal wave that extended all the way across the river—there was no way around it. It was vital that the rafts hit the wave at ninety degrees. I believe it was a week later that a commercial raft like ours got turned sideways on the wave, flipped, and trapped a couple passengers underneath who drowned before rescuers could get them out.

While taking a break one afternoon at Pittsburg Landing, Doc Blackadar gave me a ten-minute kayak lesson and then we ran some four miles of river. I got through all the rapids, but tipped over twice in flatwater when I hit the eddyline. A kayak was going to be the next outdoor toy I purchased.

Packwood called it a blue ribbon trip and now more than ever was determined to preserve the canyon. It came to pass in 1975.

Wild River Study Team in Bruneau Canyon, October 1973. *Stacy Gebhards photo; courtesy Idaho Department of Fish and Game.*

8 | Rivers, Rattlers, and Floating Rocks

THE ENTIRE COUNTY OF OWYHEE in southwest Idaho is a de facto wilderness area. Nearly everything there is remote and hard to get to. It also hides the most remarkable river canyons in North America: the Bruneau, Sheep Creek, Jarbidge, East Fork of the Owyhee, Battle Creek, and Deep Creek. In October 1973, I got another one of those "gee, somebody had to do it" assignments. It was an interagency Wild River Study Team that spent two weeks exploring the Jarbidge, West Fork of the Bruneau, Bruneau River, and Sheep Creek canyons. Our report assessed their potential as candidates for National Wild Rivers classification. They met all the criteria. Twenty-six years later, Idaho politics has still blocked any action.

We were floating the main Bruneau River canyon about two miles above Sheep Creek when I began to notice stumps of juniper that had been cut with an axe years before. This was the first evidence of any human activity since we left Indian Hot Springs at the mouth of the Jarbidge. The stumps continued for a mile until we came upon the remains of a small rock shelter on the west bank.

Scattered about were some Mason jars, a small blue enameled cook kettle, three oak barrels crushed under an old fallen juniper tree, and a galvanized five-gallon gas can with pipes fitted into each end. This was a moonshiner's camp that dated back to Prohibition days. He had cut the junipers upriver and floated them down to camp to fuel the still. It was the perfect hideout for making whiskey, except he eventually cut all the wood that was readily available. From what I saw of his plumbing materials—a galvanized pipe and a gas can for the expansion chamber, called the slag box, that is supposed to settle out impurities—it was obvious that his product was not the sipping variety destined for fancy homes on Warm Springs Avenue in Boise, but more likely to be consumed in that city's back alleys and whorehouses.

My next trip down the Bruneau was in May 1979, in a kayak at flood stage with the Bureau of Land Management (BLM) River Rangers. My son-in-law, Bob Michels, was with the kayak patrol, along with Roger Rosentretter, Winston Cheney, and Jeff King. Roger also worked as a botanist for the BLM and had discovered several rare and unrecorded plants in the Bruneau Canyon.

We were traveling self-support—all our food, tents, cook gear, first aid kits, clothes, and sleeping bags jammed into every empty space in our kayaks. This added another sixty pounds or more and restricted maneuverability quite a bit. Bob told me not to worry, I should be able to handle the Bruneau okay, even with a loaded boat. I became less assured when we arrived at Indian Hot Springs and I overheard one of them say, "Man, I didn't think it would be this high."

The indestructible plastic kayaks you see nowadays were not yet on the market. We were all paddling fiberglass boats that had a tendency to open up like a raw egg when you hit a rock. The Bruneau is not only a technical whitewater run, but once you enter the canyon, you belong to the river until it spits you out at the bottom end, especially at flood stage. There are few eddies to rest in, sheer rock cliffs at the water's edge, no opportunity to scout rapids in advance, and not many places to climb out of the canyon should you lose your boat. My knuckles were starting to whiten just a bit.

Many of the smaller rapids were completely washed out in the high water. The major ones, however, got worse and elevated one notch in the River Classification System. Class III rapids were now Class IV, and IV went to V. A Class VI is considered too dangerous to run. Five-Mile Rapids was now a series of Class IV and V drops at our water level. The entry of Five-Mile began with a huge, ugly breaking wave. As I started into it, I dug my paddle as deep as I could, hoping the undercurrent would grab the blade and pull me through. The wave took my kayak and flipped it endover like a poker chip back down into the hole, upside down. Actually this was the best position to be in. At least that's what I told the crew later, making it sound as if this was preplanned. Now the breaker couldn't hit my body, thereby lowering the surface profile. Being upside down, I was more exposed to the undercurrent which pulled me on through the wave.

"Low Profile" Approach

The river was solid mud and all Bob could see was my boat turned over, floating on down the river. He was wondering what he was going to tell Maria and the kids, when to his relief and mine, I rolled back up still in the boat. Bob had had a bad experience in Five-Mile Rapids the year previous when his kayak broached on a submerged rock and broke, pinning his legs in the front. The only throw rope was in Bob's boat, behind his seat, now underwater. His upper body was still out of the water. Somehow he was able to lever the boat with his paddle and retrieve the throw rope. Winston pulled him off the rock.

Bob was later reassigned to the BLM Cottonwood District as a seasonal river ranger on the lower Salmon River. This resulted in another invitational river patrol one summer in late August. We were camped on a sand bar in Hells Canyon at the confluence of the Salmon and Snake rivers. I had gotten up in the middle of the night to take care of an urgent biological function and was standing at the edge of the water, very appropriately, in my birthday suit. I looked at my watch. All hands were straight up, exactly midnight. With the next flick of the second hand, I would be officially one year older.

It was overcast and the clouds had taken on an eerie, incandescent glow. I could clearly make out the rugged outline of the canyon rim on the Oregon side of the river. A bolt of lightning sizzled over my head and exploded into the mountainside thirty yards above camp, setting fire to the dry grass and brush. People were scrambling for cover all over the sandbar. Where was my pile of carp when I needed them the most? I settled for a low spot in the sand, pulled a tarp over me as the rain hit, and tried to make my body as flat as possible. I peered out from under the tarp. The rain had extinguished my birthday candle, but that was one helluva match they used to light it.

The next canyon kayak trip was May 12–17, 1983, through Deep Creek and on into the East Fork of the Owyhee River. This was a business trip to collect information on lamb production of California bighorn sheep that had been reintroduced by Fish and Game. Department personnel were Andy Ogden, wildlife biologist, and conservation officers Jerry Gifford and Big John Nagel. Roger Rosentretter had been on some of the route and came along as river guide. Hydra Kayak Company loaned us plastic kayaks for what we knew would be a rocky ride for fifty-seven miles. I ended up with eighty-five pounds of gear in my boat.

As far as we knew, this was a first descent on the upper end of Deep Creek. Not a big deal, but we got to name the rapids, which were short but interesting. The chutes are ten feet long, two feet

wide, with at least two right-angle turns which are not easy to negotiate in a thirteen-foot kayak. The first one above Cow Valley we named
Watermelon Seed. You push with both hands on the rocks until it
squirts the kayak out like a seed and over the drop. Below Cow Valley is Gifford's Gulp and Big John's Wallbanger Number One. Deep
Creek was running 175 cubic feet per second and forty degrees Fahr-
enheit from the melting snows.

I thought no scenery could ever surpass the Bruneau and Sheep
Creek Canyons until we entered the Owyhee below Deep Creek—
incredible rock walls, colors, and shapes. The river from here to
Crutcher's Crossing is not too technical, as long as you portage
Rockslide Rapids where, several years previous, two canoeists got
sucked under the boulder pile and were killed. However, even the
portage is a challenge and takes two hours to maneuver.

Roger looked over the rapids, deciding he could be the first to
successfully run it and save two hours of dragging his kayak through
the rocks. He made the first fifty feet with some difficulty, avoiding
the boulder pile, then he dropped into a cauldron of water that was
surging up and down, four feet at a time. His boat got pinned against
the wall, flipped, and was unable to roll back up. Soon, a paddle
washed down the main rapids, followed by a kayak spewing out gear
and, finally, Roger.

Roger and boat washed up on an island below the rapids. As I
paddled down from the end of the portage, I anticipated having to set
a broken arm or leg. However, all he received were some scrapes on
one hand, so I took off after his paddle. After two miles of picking up
gear that had washed out of his boat, I found the paddle in an eddy.
About an hour later the crew caught up with me, Roger paddling his
kayak with two tin plates.

We stopped for lunch, then moved on to the next adventure of
the day, Bullseye Rapids, also called the Slot or Thread the Needle.
The only route was between two large boulders—a six-foot drop
through a winding sluice barely wide enough for a kayak. Big John
flipped over, bailed out, and swam for one of the boulders while his
kayak went through the slot without him. John was now standing
alone on a boulder in the middle of the river, his empty kayak eddied
out below, waiting for him to finish the run. We got a throw rope to
Big John, had him jump back into the river, and swung him over to
his kayak in the eddy. He climbed back in, went around the bend,
crashed into a wall, flipped, and swam again. I think Big John may
have set some kind of a record, swimming Bullseye Rapids three
times on a single run. Roger, in the meantime, was up on the hillside

trying to shout instructions, but the rapids were so loud we couldn't hear him nor could he hear the rattlesnake he was standing on.

I had seen Roger's footwork at the dance halls in Stanley, so it was no surprise that the rattlesnake never got a bite of him. Rattlers are fairly common in Idaho as far north as the Clearwater River, and usually limited to elevations below 5,000 feet. The biggest I've seen have been in Owyhee County, along the Nevada border, ranging thirty-six to forty-two inches in length.

My first experience with rattlesnakes was at a large denning site on the south end of Great Salt Lake in Utah, helping a student collect snakes for a graduate study. It was like a scene out of an old Hollywood jungle movie, standing there in a pile of rocks with parts of snakes sticking out of every opening. Fortunately it was early spring. The snakes were just beginning to emerge from the den and were not too active. Nevertheless, this was not the place to trip and fall. Whenever one snake began to rattle, it would set off a chain reaction of rattling that carried on down into the recesses of the den.

Due to the steep nature of Idaho terrain, snakes have a tendency to gravitate to the bottom of river canyons and creeks. Here, the vegetation is more lush, attracting rodents and insects, which are their food supply. On river trips we occasionally found a rattler sharing our campsite. Rather than kill it, we would pin the head to the ground with a stick so we could grab it tightly behind the head and toss it into the river for the current to carry it on downstream.

One place we always found snakes was the lower end of Camas Creek, where it empties into the Middle Fork of the Salmon River and from there on down to the Mormon Ranch. The creek goes through a narrow rocky gap with the creek on one side of the trail and a rock bluff rising up the other side. More than once I've ridden through there on horseback, unable to hear a snake rattling because of the creek noise, until I was right alongside and looked over to see one coiled in the rocks a few feet away at leg height. The snakes always allowed us passage, but it still raised the hair on the back of my neck every time I rode through there.

I was walking down to the river behind the Mormon Ranch one morning to catch some fish for breakfast and nearly stepped on a large rattlesnake that appeared to be in a really bad mood. Keeping an eye on the snake, I reached down for a stick so I could move him to the river and a ride downstream. As I picked up the stick, a big yellowjacket hornet stung me on the wrist—I was certain I had been bitten by another snake. Anyway, the snake escaped and I flipped that stick so high in the air, I'm not sure it ever came back down. I had lost my enthusiasm for a fish breakfast, went back to the cabin, and stirred up some beer pancakes instead.

Yet another snake incident occurred when the Bureau of Land Management conducted a demonstration tour in Owyhee County. The purpose of the tour was to show a large contingent of IDFG commissioners, supervisors, and staff biologists, along with BLM staff from the state office—about forty people—some of the BLM wildlife enhancement and range management projects. A group this large tends to lose momentum by the third day, clustering and standing around like a herd of cattle when the flies are bad. We had returned to the bus and vans after hiking in the dust for an hour to look at what was supposed to be a riparian enclosure. This is a section of stream fenced off from cattle grazing, allowing the regrowth of streamside vegetation to stabilize the banks and return the stream to a natural condition. Cows had somehow figured out how to open and pull back the wire gate, walked on in, and consumed everything that was green in color. I was bringing up the rear and happened to see a rattlesnake, so I caught it and brought it along. This was the first live animal, other than cows, we had seen in three days and I thought everyone would like to know that some native wildlife was still around. No one knew that I had picked up the snake, but as I walked into the dusty, lethargic entourage, the snake began to rattle its tail. It was like Moses parting the Red Sea. Within seconds the charter bus and three vans were filled and the doors slammed shut. There was some question whether I would get a ride back, even after I turned the snake loose.

The lower Salmon River canyon is also good snake country. Bob, my son-in-law, used to take quite a few snakes to make into hat bands and would fillet off the meat—rattlesnake is a lot like chicken when cooked, but of course, no wings or drumsticks. One evening, Bob was busy filleting snakes, when several pieces of meat had fallen to the kitchen floor. My grandson, Bobby, still in diapers, had crawled into the kitchen and begun foraging about. Bob heard a munching sound and looked down as Bobby swallowed the last piece of raw rattlesnake. It never made him sick, and in fact, the meat may have contained some kind of growth hormone—at age thirteen, he's pushing six feet. However, he did seem to slither around a lot before he learned to walk.

In 1981, I took on a new job assignment as regional supervisor for southwest Idaho, which involved all aspects of Fish and Game operations—fish and wildlife management, land management, information/education, regional office administration, volunteer programs, and conservation enforcement. One of my goals was to spend at least one day in the field with each regional employee. The newly assigned officer at Mountain Home, Jeff Wolfe, was getting an education in Owyhee County mud and its capacity to immobilize four-wheel drive vehicles. Jeff had outfitted his pickup with wooden planks, cable, come-along, steel bars, handy-man jack, and rope and vowed he would never walk out of Owyhee County again. I planned to spend a day with him to look at some new country he wanted to show me up in the mountains near the Nevada border.

Our road was little more than two cow trails through the sagebrush. Jeff had no sooner finished telling me about all his extrication equipment when the left front wheel dropped out of sight in a mud hole. I said, "Good, now you can give me a demonstration." The front of the truck was buried to the bumper on the left side. There were melting snowdrifts and the ground was too soft to hold an anchor for the come-along. The hole that the wheel went into was a spring, with water coming out and running down the road. I suggested that the only thing we could do was get some rocks down into the hole to make a solid base for the handyman jack.

We had to search a wide area, but finally had a pile of rocks that I figured would do the job. I grabbed a grapefruit-size rock and threw it into the hole. It floated on the surface like a piece of wood. What the hell was going on? Threw another one in and it floated alongside the first one. I pushed them underwater, deep into the springhole. They popped back up like corks. All the rocks we had found and gathered up, I discovered, were pumice, a volcanic cinder rock that is filled with tiny bubbles and will float in water. There was no way we were going to fill in a springhole with floating rocks.

Our position was such that we could not access any of the IDFG radio repeaters and call for assistance. Jeff said, not a problem, because he had the radio frequency of the Nevada Fish and Game and got an instant reply. He described our location, and they said there would be two officers in a truck to pull us out within an hour. Four hours later no one had showed, the Nevada office had gone off the air, and there was no radio contact with the rescue vehicle. We again tried all the IDFG radio channels, got a freak bounce, and made contact 350 miles north at Lewiston. They relayed information to the Bruneau Wildlife Area, forty miles from us, and we got pulled out at 1:00 a.m. I promised Jeff I would send him a sackful of river rocks, guaranteed to sink, to add to his emergency equipment.

The following day, I received a phone call from Nevada Fish and Game wanting to know if we could tell them where they might find the officers they sent to look for us.

A handyman jack is a wonderful device. It has rescued countless Fish and Game vehicles and their drivers from unnamed mud holes and dirt roads all over the state. I had to go check the water level in April one year at a small reservoir way off in the sagebrush. About nine miles in from the main road, I high-centered my 1962 Dodge, two-wheel drive carryall in the middle of a long mud puddle.

I found that I could lift the back of the Dodge with the handyman jack and stuff sagebrush under the back wheels. This gave enough traction, when the jack was removed, to back the truck out a foot or more each time. I was into the mudhole about twenty-five feet and needed an armful of sagebrush for every foot gained. This was not how I wanted to spend my day.

I nearly had the truck out. All I had to do now was let the jack down and I could get the rear wheels onto solid ground and back on out. But the jack wouldn't move, up or down. Too much mud had gotten into the working parts. I tried to rock the truck off the jack, but the front wheels and frame were solid in the mud. Tried pulling and kicking the jack, wouldn't move. After giving the appropriate blessing for the situation, I gave up. I said to myself, "Well, piss on it. I might as well start walking." As I was headed down the road, I thought, that might not be a bad idea. I went back to the truck, pissed on the jack, washing the mud out, let the jack down, and drove on out.

9 | Cookbook Mountain

I F EVERY COOKBOOK and recipe card written were piled in one spot, it would throw the earth off balance and out of rotation. Surely, by now, cooks have written down every possible way there is to fix eggs, meat, and beans. I didn't want to do another cookbook, but in case something might have been left out on Cookbook Mountain, I'll add a little more to the pile.

Recipes have some pretty fancy names, like chicken *bourguignonne*, *filet en croute*, *blanquette de veau*, *coquilles St. Jacques Parisienne*. Most of the camp cooks I'm acquainted with don't speak French or even very good English at times. Consequently, when a camp cook has stirred up something that everyone eats without secretly pitching it into the river or nearby brush, the new dish is christened with the name of the camp's location. It might be Selway Stew, Black Rock Omelet, or Tom's West Fork Lasagna—the creator is often included in the title if it is worth the notoriety.

Any favorite recipe that works for you at home should work on the river or in the mountains. Many ingredients can be premixed or precooked, ziplock bagged, and frozen for use several days later. A little experimentation will enhance your camp menus. Space and weight limitations can force you to simplify on prolonged trips. This is when the camp kitchen becomes a creative art studio that will produce an occasional masterpiece and lots of abstract presentations. The break point occurs around the ninth day of the trip when you are down to the stuff you had hoped you wouldn't have to use. Now they will discover whether you are a cook or not.

Ishawooa Beans

I was cooking for some sheep hunters up in the Washakie Wilderness in Wyoming, east of the Yellowstone Park boundary. Our camp was on Ishawooa Creek, which became the recipe title for the main course that evening. When I got back to Cody, somebody told me that Ishawooa was the Indian term for wolf feces. Always research the origin of your recipe titles. A dinner menu listing Wolf Shit Beans may not get many takers.

> 2 cups dried red beans
> 1 cup dried pinto beans
> 2 pounds meat chunks, browned
>   with a couple shots whiskey
> 4 cloves chopped garlic
> 1 tsp. cayenne
> 1 tsp. Cajun spice
> 1 tsp. Old Bay spice
> 1 tbs. salt
> 1 large can tomatoes
> 2 diced onions
> 1 each green and red pepper diced

Smells good to me.

Pre-soak beans overnight. Brown meat in a hot, greased skilled, add whiskey, and then steam with a lid on for about 5 minutes. Combine all ingredients in large pot and bring to a slow boil, adding water as needed, until the beans are cooked.

Base Camp Chili

The Ishawooa Bean recipe can be transformed into chili by also mixing in one tablespoon of cumin and two or three tablespoons of chili powder. For a little different flavor, try adding a diced dill pickle.

Cut Coulee Corned Beef

This is a quick meal for two people that works for dinner or breakfast and with eggs.

> 1 cup Minute Rice, cooked
> 1 can corned beef or hash
> 2 tbs. butter

Add a dash of the following seasonings to taste: salt, curry powder, cayenne, Cajun, paprika, pepper. Place butter in hot skillet, brown and heat hash by turning with spatula. Rice is served as a side dish along with fried eggs.

Dutch Oven Cornbread

1 1/2 cups yellow cornmeal
1/2 cup flour
2 eggs
1 cup buttermilk or 1 cup milk with 3 tbs. powdered buttermilk
1/4 cup shortening
1 tbs. sugar or molasses
1/2 tsp. baking soda
3 tsp. baking powder
1 tsp. salt

Mix ingredients together, place in hot greased dutch oven, cover lid with coals, and place oven over coals on the ground. Check every ten minutes. The dry ingredients can be premixed at home and put in a ziplock plastic bag.

Dutch Oven Biscuits

No special recipe is needed for these, just a box of Bisquick and some water.

Mix up the dough, shape the biscuits with some dry flour, sprinkle flour in a preheated dutch oven. Add the biscuits, leaving space for expansion. There should be coals on the lid and under the oven. Check every ten minutes or so. Cooking time for biscuits or cornbread depends on the amount of coals used and variables like air temperature and wind velocity. You'll figure out the right amount after burning one or two batches, so keep trying.

Dutch Oven Apple Crisp

6 to 10 apples sliced, or dried apples reconstituted in water
2 tbs. water
1/2 cup brown sugar
1/4 cup melted butter
1 tsp. cinnamon
1 tsp. nutmeg

Mix the above ingredients, add to dutch oven, and cook until apples are slightly soft, then add:

1 cup rolled oats mixed with 1/4 cup flour

Add coals to lid and under oven, bake until lightly browned.

Survival Sandwiches

Our camp cook, John Steile from Jerome, had kept our bellies full and satisfied during some twenty years worth of elk hunting in the Selway River Wilderness. His featured lunch item was two peanut butter sandwiches with cheese, strawberry jam, mayonnaise, and occasionally a leaf of lettuce. I could handle a peanut butter sandwich, but it had to be like my whiskey: I preferred it straight.

Steile Survival Sandwich

He would load us up each morning with the sandwiches for our hunting packs. I dared not risk a code violation and would graciously accept these gut bombs. At the end of the day when we returned to camp, he would ask how the lunches were. "Just great, John," we replied. The next day's sandwiches would be even thicker and heavier.

A person could survive for a long time on the twenty years of peanut butter sandwiches I buried on the upper Selway.

Code of the West

It's the unwritten Code of the West that if you bitch about the cooking in camp, the job is yours. At Chamberlain Basin elk camp in October 1995, I cooked a couple of meals that didn't taste right to me, but there were no comments. I even complained openly one morning about how the venison steaks for breakfast had tasted, but since I was the one who cooked them, this didn't register as a code violation. The code remained unbroken until lunch on the last day when we were breaking camp. Tom Gehring, my son-in-law, pulled out some hard-boiled eggs he had fixed that morning for us. We salted them down, took one bite, and spit them out in unison. This was the last meal and he had nothing to lose, so Wes Rose, my hunting pardner, said, "Tom, these eggs taste horrible." A little detective work by John revealed that I had failed to label a large shaker container as sugar instead of salt.

Fresh Meat in Camp

I was born with carnivore genes and can't subsist long without fresh meat or fish. I've learned not to depend on having meat hanging in camp or fish by the second day. I will wrap freezer packages of meat or fish individually with several layers of newspaper, label, and carry them in soft insulated coolers. These fit nicely in a pack box or pannier. In camp they are kept in the shade, maybe under a sleeping bag, or tied to a bush and placed in a cool stream. Meat and fish will keep for over a week this way during the summer and longer in the fall.

Elk Jerky

We were traveling as light as possible in order to climb up, what could hardly be called a trail, to the top of Scoria Creek in Wyoming. Here we would set up a spike camp at elevation 9,960 feet for the next three or four days to hunt bighorn sheep. Food staples were elk jerky and dried beans. You can't travel much lighter than that. The climb was tough, even for mules. One place around the head of a ravine was so bad I stayed on Sue, my riding mule, because I didn't think I could walk across it. Four legs would be better than my two. The rest of the mules got around, but the trail was demolished. We would have to find another route on our return.

While cooking a pot of beans for supper, I discovered that in my haste, I had forgotten my spice bag. All the salt was at base camp. It's a well-known fact among those who have traveled the backcountry with me that if you need anything in camp, I have it somewhere in my gear: needle, thread, button, shoelace, leather strap, copper rivets, Conway buckle, extra cinch, mule shoe, halter rope, whatever. The two hunters that Wes had invited from Oregon always needed something. I always had it. This became an obsession with them: Find something I couldn't fix or come up with. When they heard that I didn't have the salt, I could see Cliff and Hawk exchanging glances with each other. Now they had me—the salt was three-and-a-half hours and five miles back down the mountain.

I dug around in my first aid kit and found a bottle of salt tablets. Incidentally, a salt tablet or half teaspoon of salt in a glass of water can relieve a severe muscle cramp in one or two minutes for me. I mashed up some tablets, administered first aid, and saved what otherwise would have been a terminal pot of beans. My reputation was so far untarnished.

Take 2 of these and call me in the morning.

SALT TABS

Another item I keep in my first aid kit is a tube of Desitin. Many parents with babies have used this product for treating diaper rash. For years I had suffered with cracking calluses and fingertips from pulling ropes and latigos on pack trips. Nothing had ever worked, except time, to heal the wounds until I found that Desitin also was good for the hands as well as butts. Unfortunately this discovery will never gain popularity in the West. How many mule packers or tough, old cowboys do you think would risk being seen pulling diaper rash ointment out of their saddle bags at the end of the day?

The next morning, Cliff was acting surly. He'd been digging in his teeth with a sharpened stick for an hour trying to dislodge a piece of elk jerky. Finally in desperation he said smugly, "Well, what do you do in a place like this when you don't have any dental floss?" I reached into my shirt pocket, pulled out a box of dental floss, and cut him off a piece.

The jerky recipe was a simple marinade in which 1/4-inch meat strips, cut across the grain with all the fat removed, are soaked overnight in the refrigerator:

    1 cup soy sauce
    1/3 cup red wine
    1/3 cup molasses
    3 tbs. finely chopped ginger root
    3 cloves chopped garlic
    1 tbs. Worcestershire
    1 1/2 lbs. meat strips
    1/2 tsp. Liquid Smoke (if using a food dehydrator)

Drain excess marinade by placing meat in colander. Then place strips on paper towels and pat dry. Sprinkle meat with coarse black pepper and place on smoker racks. Try variations on flavors with other spices if you don't like this one.

Beer Pancakes

    2 cups pancake mix
    1/3 cup milk
    1 can of beer (any type will do)
    1 tbs. oil
    2 eggs

I make the batter fairly thin, as the beer tends to give the pancakes a higher rise. The milk helps to hold the cake together when flipping and assures some extra leftover beer for the cook.

Mountain Seafood

The dry fly settled slowly on the crystal water of the Salmon's Middle Fork, drifted along a sheer rock wall, and was swallowed instantly in an explosion of foam and fish. A six-foot graphite rod was put to the test and the fisherman cried, "That has to be the biggest cutthroat we've hooked yet." On one end of the rod was a nationally known fly fisherman and Henry's Fork guide, Will Godfrey. On the end of his dry fly was not the regal westslope cutthroat we had been catching, but *Ptychocheilus oregonensis*, the northern squawfish.

Until he came over the side of the raft, the squawfish had successfully fooled everyone into thinking he was a sporty fish, an opponent worthy to challenge the skills of a master fly fisherman. Indeed, my friend had to admit he was impressed with the squawfish, although not its looks. When I suggested that he would be even more impressed after eating it, he looked at me as though I had spent too many days on the river with my hat off.

Squawfish are a native western minnow. Four distinct species have been described: the northern squawfish, which ranges throughout the Columbia River basin into Canada and Montana; the Sacramento squawfish; the Umpqua squawfish in Oregon; and the Colorado squawfish, recognized as the largest of the American minnows, reaching lengths of five feet and weighing up to eighty pounds. Damming (more correctly damning) of the Colorado and loss of river environment has put this fish on the Endangered Species List. Efforts are under way to artificially rear the Colorado squawfish in hatcheries to insure its preservation.

There is little chance that the northern squawfish will ever be threatened, since it readily adapts to environmental change. They can spawn prolifically in streams, lakes, and reservoirs and are found from warm, low elevation streams to cold, high elevation headwaters. Spawning generally occurs in July with eggs hatching within four days in warmer waters.

Prior to the influence and prejudices of modern-day fishermen, squawfish were a staple foodfish of western Indian tribes. I was on a Snake River float trip with a group of canoers and caught a dozen big squawfish. No one could understand why I was keeping such trash fish. Dinner that evening was to be rib steaks grilled over the campfire. I went ahead and fried up some of the squawfish for everyone to nibble on before supper. Next thing I knew, the appetizers became the main course and the steaks went back into the coolers for breakfast.

Discounting its looks—something like an unemployed prize-fighter—the only problem you have to overcome in preparation are the small fishbones. All fishes in the minnow and sucker families have numerous floating intramuscular bones. The first step is to fillet the meat off the bones, leaving the skin intact. This can be done without first gutting the fish. Place the fillet skin-side down on a cutting board and run a thin-bladed knife between the skin and muscle. Cut into 3/8-inch strips by cutting crosswise to the length of the fillet. Since the bones lie lengthwise in the fillet, this reduces these fine bones to no longer than 3/8-inch. This same technique is used in preparation of carp and suckers for deep-frying.

Now all you need is a one-to-one mixture of cornmeal and Wondra flour,* a skillet, hot cooking oil, and some skeptical fish eaters. Roll the fish sticks in the meal and deep-fry until golden brown. Salt and spice to taste. Frying will cook the bones to the extent they are hardly noticeable. You will find, as I have on many riverside fish fries, that you didn't cook enough, and your skeptics will come back for seconds, digging through smallmouth bass and trout to find one more piece of squawfish.

Hells Canyon Batter

This is one I learned from the cook at Willow Creek Camp during the trip with Burl Ives. It works great with carp fish sticks (keep them under 3/8 inch to reduce bone length) and has passed the taste test of maybe thousands of fish eaters. Also works with any recipe calling for a deep-fry batter such as onion rings or shrimp. Don't overheat the cooking oil. This will cook the batter too quickly and not allow the fish to cook through.

Mix:
1 cup cold water
1 egg
1/4 cup salad oil
Add:
1 cup Wondra flour
4 tsp. cornstarch
1 tsp. baking powder
1 tsp. salt
1/2 tsp. MSG, optional

---

*I use Wondra flour in all cooking for fish or as a coating for browning meats. It is a mixture of wheat and malted barley. I find that it does not milk into the oil during frying and seems to cling better.

Sandy's Red Sauce

This makes an excellent addition to deep-fried carp and is superior to any shrimp cocktail sauce you can buy in the store.

1 cup catsup
1 cup chili sauce
1/2 tsp. Tabasco
1/2 tsp. Worcestershire
1/2 juiced lemon
3 tbs. ground (not creamed) horseradish

Sandy's Tartar Sauce

1 cup (real) mayonnaise
2 tsp. Dijon mustard
1 tsp. parsley
1 diced dill pickle
1 tbs. diced onion
1 tsp. vinegar with 1/2 tsp. tarragon
dash Tabasco and Worcestershire
juice of lemon to taste

Seviche

6 cups chopped raw fish (I use only trout or whitefish)
3 cups chopped onions
3 cups chopped tomatoes
1 cup diced chilies
15 diced green olives
4 cloves chopped garlic
1 1/2 tbs. salt
2 tsp. Tabasco
1 tbs. olive oil
3 tsp. catsup

Refrigerate fish covered in lemon juice overnight, then drain off most of the juice. Mix with remaining ingredients. Marinate for at least four hours in refrigerator. Serve with crackers.

Pickled Fish

Fillet trout or whitefish, remove skin, cut into two-inch chunks. Soak twelve hours in refrigerator in a brine made with one cup pickling salt for each quart of water.

Sour Pickled: Pour off brine, rinse in cold water. Layer fish in a gallon jar, covered with slices of white onion, garlic, carrot, celery, occasional red pepper, lemon (peeled), and sprinkle with pickling spice. Alternate layers in that order. Cover with half water/half white vinegar. Refrigerate one week and eat.

Sweet Pickled: Pour off brine, soak in white vinegar in refrigerator for twenty-four hours. Remove and layer in jar with slices of white onion. Add liquor and refrigerate for two weeks.

Liquor is prepared by bringing to a boil and simmering one-half hour:

1 cup white vinegar
1/2 cup water
1/2 cup sugar
3 tsp. pickling spice
12 whole allspice
Cool and add 1/2 cup of white port wine.
You can also add sour cream after the fish have pickled for two weeks.

Smoked Fish: Salmon, Steelhead, Trout, Whitefish, Carp

I messed around for years with different brine recipes that require soaking overnight and found the simple way is the best way. Fillet fish, leaving skin on. A large fish, such as salmon or steelhead, is filleted and cut crosswise into one-inch fish sticks. For trout and whitefish, leave the fillet whole. Rinse the fish in cold water and then dredge in a bowl containing Morton's Sugar Cure. Discard the envelope containing curing spices. If you can't find this in a store, try mixing 1/2 cup brown sugar with one cup pickling salt. Add a layer of Sugar Cure in a porcelain broiler pan. Place fish on this and cover with more Sugar Cure. Leave exposed to room temperature for forty-five minutes then rinse thoroughly in cold water, allowing water to drain. Lay out on paper towels and pat dry. Fish can now be placed on smoking trays, skin side down. Adjust saltiness of the fish by the amount of time it is in the salt/sugar mixture. Thinner fillets will take less time.

Fresh Fish

If someone brings you a mess of trout they just caught and wants them cooked up, try to talk them into waiting until tomorrow. If they still insist, then fillet the fish to remove the backbone, shave off the skin, and cut into two-inch chunks. Otherwise, your fresh fish will coil up like a clockspring as it fries. This does not affect the taste but will put the cook in a tense mood while trying to brown a fish on each side that is shaped like a giant wood screw in the frying pan. Better yet, keep it cool and dry until the next day. It will still taste as good as fresh caught.

I prefer to fillet all my trout over eight inches long and roll in the standard one-to-one yellow cornmeal/Wondra flour mix. A good fish seasoning is Old Bay, but if you want to up the ante, use Cajun seasoning or cayenne with it. Whitefish are also great filleted and fried, but remove the skin after filleting.

Fillet Parmesan: Trout, Whitefish, Perch, Crappie, Bass

    2 eggs
    1/3 cup milk
    1 tsp. minced garlic
    4 green onions/stems, chopped fine
    3/4 cup fresh shredded Parmesan or Romano cheese
Mix eggs and milk and then the remainder of ingredients. Wet fillets in water and roll in Wondra flour. Dip fillets in the egg batter and place in a skillet with a pat of butter at medium heat—a Teflon-covered skillet works best. More of the batter can be put on the fish, if needed, after they are in the pan. Before turning fillets, season with Old Bay, Cajun, salt, and cayenne. Fillets should be 3/8 inch or less in thickness. The egg batter will brown quickly, so heat must be carefully controlled to allow fish to cook through.

Rocky Mountain Oysters

Anyone will tell you, the only time these oysters are found in water is when a band of sheep are crossing a stream or a herd of cattle swimming a river. But there really is a Rocky Mountain oyster—well sort of—that lives in cold mountain streams and rivers. It is the native black-shelled freshwater mussel, *genus Margaritifera*, not to be confused with a smaller, tan-colored exotic, the Asiatic clam. Mussels were an important food item among the Indians of the Pacific Northwest. Large mounds of discarded mussel shells can still be found adjacent to ancient Indian campsites.

Mussels that are up to six or seven inches in length can be eighty years of age and tough as a rubber truck tire when cooked. Those that are one to three inches long aren't bad if diced and boiled or steamed in the shell in foil by the campfire. I would not rate them as a gourmet item. I did, however, utilize mussels to supplement a rather meager food supply on a Selway River float trip in 1974. In addition to not bringing much in the way of groceries, the person in charge of the trip failed to bring cooking oil, flour, or a pancake turner, which was academic anyway, since he had no skillet. Other omissions were butter for corn-on-the-cob, rain gear, and tents for his crew.

I had a premonition as we went through Lolo, Montana, on the way in and purchased a can of coffee, thereby avoiding what would have been a serious mutiny on down the river. It rained during most of the trip, and I was the only person who brought a small waterproof tarp. I asked Ron, the crew leader, as we loaded the truck at the Selway Falls takeout, why he didn't bring any tents or rain gear. He said, "We were on the river for eight days last year, and it didn't rain a drop."

We've gobbled up lots of mammalian oysters (elk, moose, and deer) in hunting camps as well. Just cut and peel off the exterior membrane, slice, roll in Wondra flour, and brown in a skillet with some butter. Since there are only two oysters per animal—and not even that if it's a cow or doe hunt—don't plan to feed a large party. The finest Rocky Mountain oysters I have ever eaten, by the way, were at the Proud Cut Saloon in Cody, Wyoming.

River Of No Return Oysters

Your next option is to resort to regular saltwater oysters that you take to the backcountry in a tin can. If you are unable to find a good recipe on Cookbook Mountain, you can use the one that I improvised in elk camp.

> 3 cans oysters (8 oz)
> 2 cans chopped clams (6.5 oz)
> 3 potatoes, diced and boiled
> 3 cups water
> 2 handfuls dried milk
> 1 handful Wondra flour
> 1/2 pound bacon, fried crisp and diced
> 2 tbs. butter
> Some dried morel mushrooms, presoaked and drained
> 3 cloves garlic, chopped
> 1 small onion, chopped (onion and garlic sautéed together)
> 4 to 5 dashes cayenne
> 2 tsp. Old Bay
> 2 tsp. salt
> 1 tsp. coarse black pepper

Add liquid from oysters and clams to water and milk, then add other ingredients and heat to below boiling. Simmer ten minutes, add oysters and clams, simmer another ten.

Cooking with Wine

This is for the cook to drink while preparing the meal.

    1 quart of packed dandelion blossoms, all stems removed
    1 gallon water
    6 cups sugar
    1/2 cup honey
    1 cup strong black tea
    Juice of 3 lemons
    1 pound raisins
    1 package baker's yeast

Dissolve sugar in boiling water and add honey, tea, and lemon. Pour this while hot over the dandelions in a stainless steel or heavy plastic container. Mix in yeast after it cools. Strain off blossoms on the third day, otherwise the wine will be bitter. Place in glass jug, add whole raisins, and attach fermentation trap or cork loosely. It's ready to drink when you start cutting up your elk.

Dandelion is by far the best wine I've made. When the kids were little, I would pay them twenty-five cents a quart for the picked blossoms. I didn't find out until years later they had subcontracted the picking with other kids in the neighborhood for a much lower price. I experimented with vegetables for a while and made some interesting wines from red beets, carrots, tomatoes, onions (this one had to age over a year before you could drink it), potatoes, and spinach (honest, I did).

One winter I tried out a recipe for corn wine that had cracked corn and raisins as the primary ingredient, along with oranges, lemons, peppercorns, sugar, yeast, and water. The initial fermentation was around two weeks, after which the liquid was strained off and placed in gallon jugs with a water seal for the second, or anaerobic, fermentation stage.

The leftover cracked corn and raisins I put in a canner kettle and placed out in the backyard under a tree. I didn't want to feed it to my horse Smokey, as it was saturated with fermenting liquid that was probably over 12 percent alcohol. I told Maria I would dispose of it when I got back from a meeting down in northern Utah. A big snowstorm closed the highways and I was stranded in Pocatello, unable to get back to Boise the next day. I called home to see how things were going. Maria wanted to know how much money was left in the checking account and informed me that I might be purchasing a flock of Guinea hens when I got back.

Our neighbor, across the road, operated a small farm and milked a few cows. He also owned a flock of Guinea hens that foraged all over like a pack of hungry coyotes and were just as intimidating. The afternoon of the snowstorm, Maria looked out in the backyard to see the flock of birds circled around the canner kettle with their heads buried in the corn mash. She tried to shoo them off, but they were not about to leave anything this good.

By the time the kids got home from school, the kettle was empty and several birds had flown up to the top of our big locust tree. The remainder lined up on the top rail of the pole fence around the backyard to relax and digest their "corn mash cocktail." The kids were looking out the back window at the falling snow and the birds, when one of them toppled out of the locust tree and hit the ground. Two more fell out of the tree as the birds on the rail fence began to keel over, one by one, until the entire flock was passed out on the snow.

The kids began loading the drunken Guinea hens into their little red wagon and hauling them over to the farmhouse. I got home the next day and waited for a call from the farmer to tell me how much money I owed him. I was certain this would not be covered on my homeowner's liability insurance policy. I thought, maybe, I could at least file a claim for the feed they had eaten.

The following morning, I still had not received a phone call. The birds had been placed in the milking shed, probably to keep them from freezing solid, which would have made them difficult to dress out. I was fixing breakfast coffee as I looked out the kitchen window. The sun was just coming up, frost crystals were floating in the air. Across the road, the farmer headed for the milking shed, opened the door, and was nearly flattened by a flying stampede of Guinea hens that sailed across the field, landing in our backyard somewhat shaky and red-eyed and began searching under every tree for another kettle of corn mash.

Camassia Quamash

If it had been my choice, the blue camas would be the Idaho state flower, not the syringa. Although the syringa is a nice white-flowering, fragrant shrub and has been domesticated for landscaping our homes, and the straight limbs were used by Indians as arrow shafts, it does not carry the historical credentials of the camas. This plant has been a staple in the diet of Indians throughout the Pacific Northwest for thousands of years. A few trappers and settlers may have been run through by syringa arrows, but far more were saved from starvation by the onion-like bulbs of the camas.

So vital were the moist meadows and high prairies where it grew in profusion, that Indian tribes often fought each other for harvesting rights. The camas was the centerpiece of the Nez Perce and Bannock Indian Wars of Idaho in 1877 and 1878 after the tribes were denied access by the U.S. Government to their historic digging sites. Settlers were turning loose great numbers of hogs to root out and consume Indian tradition and critical food supplies. Plows soon overturned the camas prairies and meadows for cultivation.

In the short span of some 125 years, "civilized" man has methodically pushed the blue camas to a remnant status in much the same way as he has nearly exterminated the great runs of salmon and steelhead in the Pacific Northwest by altering the habitat of plants and animals alike.

Camas bulbs are one of my favorite wild foods, surpassed only by the morel mushroom. They should be dug during the flowering

Blue
Camas

stage, in the late spring, so you can differentiate them from death camas, *genus Zygadenus,* which may grow in close proximity, but usually in a drier site. The camas flower is a bright blue-purple. From a distance, a meadow full of camas may appear as a pond of blue water. Occasionally, a white variant of the flower will stand out in contrast.

Death camas flowers a little later, with short greenish-white or cream-colored petals. Its bulb is very similar to those of the wild onion, sego lily, wild hyacinth, and camas, all of which are edible. But, the death camas contains poisonous alkaloids that can be twice as toxic as strychnine. This will hopefully dampen the enthusiasm of novice root-diggers, who start collecting and eating wild plants without careful study and close examination of their menus.

I enjoy camas bulbs raw, boiled, mashed and fried, or baked in foil by a campfire. One pound of fresh bulbs contains some 500 Kcal in carbohydrates, protein, and a small amount of fat. I would caution against consuming large quantities. My experience with it would place the gas producing potential at about ten times that of an equal amount of beans. This was also noted in the Journals of Lewis and Clark on October 7, 1805, by Captain Clark who wrote: "Capt Lewis & my Self ate a supper of roots (camas) boiled, which filled us So full of wind, that we were Scarcely able to Breathe . . . . all night felt the effects of it." Eating camas should be reserved for outdoor, backcountry camps. It is not compatible with confined, populated spaces such as a church or an elevator.

Field Care and Storage of Fish and Game Meat

An entire library of cookbooks and a French chef cannot salvage a trout fillet or a venison tenderloin if it's not properly cared for in the field. Trout should be gutted soon after catching and placed in a cooler, not immersed in water on a stringer for the next three hours. If a cooler is not available and you have a creel, the gutted fish should be layered in between grass. In a camp situation, unless you have access to snow, try to cook fish within twenty-four hours.

Say in June you catch some nice red-meated trout, or a friend gives you some fresh salmon from the coast. You put it in a plastic bag or wrap it in aluminum foil and stick it in the freezer. During December you invite guests over for a fish dinner. You thaw the fish out. It looks like it has already been cooked on the outside and smells so strong it makes your eyes water. How can this happen? The fish has been in a freezer for six months at ten degrees below zero.

First, the wrapping has not provided a barrier to evaporation and the exterior tissues have dehydrated or freezer burned. Secondly, the inadequate wrapping has allowed oxygen to react chemically with the unsaturated fatty acids in the fish oil. This oxidation produces ketones, aldehydes, and acids that smell bad and taste worse.

Poorly wrapped fish with moderate to high oil content, 5 to 10 percent, can become rancid in three months while frozen. Fish with high oil content include salmon, steelhead, kokanee, red-meated trout, and catfish. Fish with low oil content, such as perch, bass, crappie, can be stored two or three times longer.

Here's how to make your catches end up on your plate instead of the cat's:

- keep freezer temperature below zero degrees
- date packages and practice first in, first out
- wrap fish in plastic wrap and double wrap in freezer paper, or freeze fillets in milk carton filled with water
- large whole fish should be frozen, dipped in water several times to form an ice glaze before wrapping.

Some big game archery seasons may begin in August. Even October seasons may experience temperatures in the high eighties. How can you keep deer or elk from spoiling when you are days away from a refrigerated meat storage facility? After gutting, the animal should be skinned and hung off the ground to allow rapid cooling. Elk or moose will need to be cut into quarters. Big game animals should never be allowed to remain unskinned, lying on the ground, and left to be processed the next day. If you have to, finish the job by flashlight or campfire. Meat that has become excessively dirty or exposed to the paunch contents can be cleaned in a nearby creek, with buckets of water at camp, or high pressure hose and brush at home.

Flies will be a problem during early season hunts, so be sure to carry meat sacks in your hunting pack. Purchase a good set of bags that will be large enough and inspect them before you leave home. A lot of meat bags, the cheap ones, are junk, so beware. If some of your meat does get fly-blown with tiny oblong white eggs, don't think it is all ruined. These can be trimmed off with a knife.

We have kept elk quarters in camp during hot weather in the Selway in September for over a week. Meat will not keep as well in warm weather if it has been boned out. This exposes it to more bacteria and increases in temperature. At night, mountain temperatures will cool and meat sacks are removed. Then in the morning we replace the meat sacks. If the daytime temperatures are apt to get excessively warm, take the quarters down from the meat pole and place them all in one pile on a canvas manty. Another manty is placed over the meat and our sleeping bags on top to insulate the pile. At night, the meat is uncovered and hung on the meat pole.

I prefer to hang and age big game for at least ten days or longer before it is cut and wrapped. I haven't let a butcher do my meat in over thirty years. It's not that difficult and you will end up with a superior product. By deboning the meat and trimming off all the fat, you eliminate any portions that may turn rancid through fat oxidation during prolonged storage. Portions are then wrapped in clear plastic and double wrapped in freezer paper.

How long can game meat be kept in a freezer if packaged this way? In September 1987 my daughter Sandy and her husband, Bryon Breen, hiked into our camp on the upper Selway to hunt elk with us. Two days later, Wes got Bryon onto a big six-point bugling bull that was in charge of a herd of cows. This had to be a traumatic experience for him, because I don't think he'd ever shot anything larger than a mallard duck.

When we were butchering the elk, Sandy was working on a hind quarter and found a 30.06 bullet encased in cartilage. The femur bone had been completely broken in two by the bullet and was held together by a thick layer of cartilage. The old bull had not only survived a serious wound, gone through at least one winter, but was back in business doing what bull elk do in the month of September.

Eight years later, Sandy was cleaning out her freezer. There at the bottom was a large package labeled "Elk Roast—87." I've read stories about archaeologists or old gold miners eating the meat of preserved mastodon carcasses that emerged from glaciers 15,000 years later. Well, the elk didn't quite fall into that category, but eight years in a freezer was a pretty long time. The exterior had dehydrated a little, but, trimmed off, the interior meat was red and firm. I cut off a steak, fried it with some butter and chopped garlic, and it tasted great. I cut the remainder of the roast into steaks, repackaged it, and gave them back to Sandy labeled, "Mastodon Steaks—95. Best If Used Before Jan. 3005."

Sell By
JAN 3005

10 | **Backcountry Citizenry**

Lunch Is on Me

IN March 1965, I was part of a search team sent to Rocky Bar, a ghost town in the mountains north of Featherville. Rocky Bar was snowbound for at least five months out of the year. Charlie Sprittles, who was in his eighties, ran a little store and hand-operated pump gas station during the summer and fall. Charlie claimed to be the town mayor elected by unanimous vote, his. He was the only permanent resident and would usually stay on through the winter.

Fish and Game would check on elk wintering conditions by snow cat on the South Fork of the Boise River. If Charlie was known to be at Rocky Bar, we would make a run up to see how he was doing and drop some fresh groceries. This year, the word was he had wintered down in the valley. In March some inquiries were made to the Elmore County sheriff about Charlie's whereabouts. Two hunters reported giving him a ride in late November from Featherville in their truck, but were stopped by snow drifts some three miles short of Rocky Bar. Charlie said he could make it the rest of the way on foot. A flyover of the town showed no signs of smoke or tracks around Charlie's store. The sheriff decided to send a ground party in.

We unloaded the Frandee SnoCat at Anderson Dam, arriving at the Fish and Game cabin in Featherville that evening in a blizzard. The next morning it was still laying down one inch of snow an hour, stopping that evening with two feet of new snow. We stayed in the cabin and played poker—not much else you can do in a deserted town during a spring blizzard. The following day was consumed with shoveling through small avalanches that had piled onto the Rocky Bar road and replacing the tracks on the snocat which came off every couple miles. We were confident we could get to Rocky Bar on the fourth day. At noon, the track came off again about three miles from town. After eating lunch on the snow, Dale Baird, a conservation officer from Glenns Ferry, and I volunteered to snowshoe in while the other members worked on replacing the track.

Dale and I forced our way into the store, found no trace of Charlie or evidence that he had been there that winter. The sheriff came back in May for another search after most of the snow had melted. He found Charlie's body in the middle of the road, three miles from town, apparently the victim of a heart attack. There was one curious aspect about the scene. The sheriff couldn't understand why there were orange peelings scattered all around the body. This was the exact location that the snocat had broken down. Lunch had "been on Charlie" that day in March.

Mental Telepathy

Idaho has had its share of other colorful backcountry residents: Buckskin Bill, The Ridgerunner, Free-Press Francis, Dugout Dick, and many others who have been the subjects of several books. They did miss recording one that I ran into in late August 1957, on the lower end of Panther Creek.

It was a hot day and I had run out of drinking water while doing a salmon spawning survey. I was not about to drink out of Panther Creek, aware of the toxic mine effluent running into it above Cobalt. Nearby was a small stream that looked alright. I was bent over to get a drink, when someone on the bank above me said, "Don't drink that water; I've got some up here at my cabin." I figured he must know something about this stream that I didn't, so I said, "Okay, I'll be right up." The cabin was made of tree limbs, four feet wide and three feet high. He reached inside, pulled out a crusty looking ceramic jug with a dirty rag stuck in the top, and handed it to me. Said, "My name's Shoup, what's yours?" I answered hesitatingly, "Gebhards, and thanks for the water, but I'm really not very thirsty." Then he began rambling on about reading the Good Book in the cool of his cabin (it had to be 110 degrees in there), and shooting rattlesnakes off rocks that were out in the middle of the creek below while voices were giving him and the snakes directions on what to do. Shoup told me that if the snake was coiled too tightly, the voice would tell it to lift its head a little bit higher and then he would blow it off.

By this time, I was starting to back up rapidly toward the road and the safety of my truck. Shoup asked me which way I was headed back to Salmon. I told him, up Panther Creek and then over Napias Creek. He went on to explain that he had a mare to be bred and was interested to know if a black horse at the ranch on Napias Creek was a stallion or gelding. Then he asked if I had any experience using mental telepathy. I had to admit I hadn't, but he said that wouldn't matter. When I went by the corral on Napias Creek, I was supposed to look between the legs of the black horse, see if he had any nuts, and let him know by mental telepathy.

I was making pretty fast tracks to my truck when Shoup hollered at me, "What did you say your name was?" I told him again. He said, "Gebhards, Gebhards, I'll be hearing you on the air." Half an hour later when I drove by the corral on Napias Creek, all the horses were in the barn, and all I transmitted was "Gebhards to Shoup: horses in the barn, unable to verify nuts, over and out."

I never did go back to see if he got my message. You couldn't be certain what the other voices might be telling him to shoot at on that particular day.

Fool's Gold

The end of August 1959, Walt Browne and I led two packhorses into upper Wilson Creek, tributary to the Middle Fork of the Salmon River, to hunt bighorn sheep. Our base camp was an old mining claim that had been developed by Snowshoe Johnson. Story was that he would spend his time during the summer in the saloons in Salmon, showing off some high-grade gold ore that he supposedly had recently discovered in his mine. All he needed to find the Mother Lode was more operating funds. He would get someone to grubstake him for the winter as a partner, go back to Wilson Creek, and come out after snowmelt in the spring. Then it was back to the saloons in Salmon to mine for some more gold.

Snowshoe may have been a backcountry con man, but he wasn't lazy. His cabin had long fallen down under winter snows, but there still remained a forge and bellows, equipment that had been hand-forged, an old riding saddle, purple whiskey bottles, miner's picks, an ore car, and a pile of broken quartz rock. If there was a mine shaft, we sure couldn't find it. Maybe it's another one of those legendary lost gold mines, or maybe it was all props for the suckers who grubstaked him.

This is not easy country to get around in. I completely destroyed a brand new pair of leather boots in ten days on the sheep hunt. We would leave camp, climb straight up for four hours, and still hear the bell on Smokey while he grazed at camp. There was a hot springs next to the creek, and it required many hours of soaking to rearrange our muscles when we got back. We did get two nice bighorn rams, the finest game meat there is for eating. Wished we could have shared some with old Snowshoe, as I'm sure he would have been an interesting person to meet—he might have even made us rich.

Early Morning Ecstasy

We were setting up a new camp on the West Fork. John picked up the shovel and wanted to know how big I wanted the hole for the latrine. I said, "Just gauge it on the amount of food we brought in." When he finished digging, I walked over to inspect it. From the size of the hole, he must have thought the entire 960 pounds of gear we packed in was food. I considered tying a rope to a tree as a rescue line in case someone fell in while using the latrine.

Size of the hole, however, was not the special feature of our camp latrines. The hunting journal entry for September 23, 1986, reads,

> Backcountry living, in time, will surface the innate creativity of a person. Put up with an inconvenience long enough and you will ultimately figure out a way to eliminate it. Such is the Surprise Creek Latrine, certainly not a facility you are apt to write home about. It consists of a rectangular hole, about 18 inches deep, spanned with two parallel logs that are extremely cold and uncomfortable in the early morning hours.
>
> I had reached my limit of endurance with this torture device, so I split two slats of firewood that would make a seat across the logs. My intent was to install the seat first thing this morning. As the sheepherder stove began to warm at 4:30 AM, I thought why not heat the slats in the oven first and take them to the woods on my morning call.
>
> Anyone who has ever had to melt frost crystals with his bare ass can fully appreciate the ultimate ecstasy of a heated toilet seat on a cold, dark morning. The Surprise Creek Latrine is suddenly a place to savor and truly write home about.

11 | Beaver Fever

I T WAS LATE AUGUST 1976. John and I hiked up Goat Creek to Joe Leonard's camp in the Sawtooths to spend the weekend. I didn't pack a canteen because I knew all I had to do was stick my face in the crystal waters that came from the snowbanks high on the mountain. Joe and Sheila were guiding some fishermen, so we made ourselves at home in the big wall tent. It had started to cool off and a fire in the sheepherder stove would feel good. All the firewood we could find was damp and we had no kindling, paper, or lighter fluid to get it started. I poured a little 120 proof moonshine whiskey on the wood, lit a match, and in ten minutes the sheepherder stove was glowing cherry-red.

These days, few people appreciate the utility of old-time corn whiskey, or "white lightning." It was the basic and common ingredient for most of the tonics and medicines that country folks depended upon. I think the stories of it being used as a snake bite medicine are exaggerated, although if you consumed more than a couple good slugs of it, you wouldn't even know if you'd been snake-bit. I used it a lot as an antiseptic on the kids and myself for cuts, abrasions, pulling out splinters, blisters—it did have a healing quality about it. I treated an open wound on Smokey's back where another horse had bitten him. It was bad enough that I couldn't put a saddle on him. After three days of moonshine medicine, it was healed and starting to hair over. I don't think it helped the hair grow, but if I lose any more, I may have to give it a try.

A week after I got back from the Sawtooths, I came down with chronic diarrhea that lasted for ten days. The doctor prescribed a variety of medicines, but none worked. Eventually it subsided and we headed for the Selway-Bitterroot Wilderness on our annual elk hunt. Opening morning I was hunting alone, had climbed a mountain, and was three miles from camp. I started to get chilled and had severe stomach cramps. I laid down on a bunch of bear grass and passed out.

An hour later I came to, rain falling on my face. I started back down the mountain for camp when the first explosive bout of diarrhea came on. This would hit me every fifteen minutes or so. Halfway down, I laid back into the slope and passed out again, waking a short time later as I started vomiting. Now I was losing fluids at both ends. I was fortunate to have the river when I got to the bottom. At times, I could only move on my hands and knees, and arrived in camp long after dark. It had taken six hours to get off the mountain.

I was a complete basket case for the next five days. The only food I could keep down was broth my hunting partners made by boiling grouse. We were twenty-five miles into the wilderness and I wasn't going anywhere until I could get up into the saddle. About the seventh day, I had recovered some and we packed up. I had another attack when I got back to Boise. This time the doctor diagnosed the problem: *Giardia lamblia*. I had lost twenty-five pounds.

The year was 1681 A.D.; the place, Delft, Holland; Anton Leeuwenhoek had completed assembly of the first microscope and described a living organism in his own stool sample. He had not only invented the world's most useful instrument for diagnosis of disease, but had unknowingly observed the very parasite that was the cause of his gastric distress—a unicellular protozoan we now call *Giardia*.

For the next 280 years little attention was given to *Giardia* other than its historic notoriety as being the first microorganism seen by human eyes. It can be found on every continent. Giardiasis is recognized as one of the most prevalent waterborne diseases and intestinal parasites in the United States. Let's follow this ubiquitous little critter through its life cycle, starting with the infectious stage. In this form, it is a tough, encapsulated oval cyst, seven by twelve microns in size. You could place about 16,500 of these cysts on the head of a pin. The thick protective coating around the cyst allows it to survive 40 degree F mountain stream waters for up to three months, water temperature of 70 degrees for one month, and 98 degrees for four days. High elevation mountain lakes and streams, therefore, are a more favorable environment for survival of the *Giardia* cyst.

In order to continue its life cycle, the cyst must be ingested by a warm-blooded animal: coyote, dog, cat, sheep, cow, elk, vole, mouse, or marmots. In fact, any mammal that consumes water contaminated with the cysts becomes a likely host. Because of their continual association with water, muskrats and beaver are the primary vector in mountain areas. Hence the label Beaver Fever. You have to wonder if the stomach disorders so often recorded in trapper and explorer journals might not have been related to the high populations of beaver that prevailed in the early 1800s.

When the cyst reaches the stomach, acidic conditions cause the protective capsule shell to be shed and a free-swimming form called the trophozoite, emerges. It must move quickly out of the stomach acid to survive and establishes residence in the upper small intestine. Here it attaches to the intestinal wall with an adhesive sucking disc and immediately commences the reproductive cycle.

Within thirty minutes, the single trophozoite divides in two during asexual reproduction. If binary multiplication continues at this pace, theoretically one organism would produce one million within ten hours and in another five hours, there could be one billion. Drinking water heavily loaded with cysts would rapidly accelerate colonization of the small intestine and onset of the disease.

In severe cases, every single cell of the epithelium, the tissue lining the small intestine, may have a trophozoite attached to it. This interferes with digestion of food, absorption of fats, vitamins, and other nutrients within the small intestine, and victims may suffer significant weight loss. I do not recommend it, however, as a weight-loss program.

Trophozoites passed onto the large intestine may reform back into the encapsulated cyst before release in the stool. In an extreme infection in humans, a single stool could contain several billion cysts, in a moderate infection, 300 million. A single stool of a beaver could carry several million infective cysts.

A 1980 study of seventy-four *Giardia* cases in Idaho found 45 percent of the patients had drunk stream water, 15 percent water from springs, and 12 percent lake water; 12 percent were swimmers. It was interesting that 16 percent had never left town and had no known exposure to unfiltered water. Cysts may survive a short period of time out of host or a water environment. Thus, they may be passed on to another host by contact with unwashed hands or contaminated clothing.

In the old days, outfitters on the Middle Fork of the Salmon River would routinely issue Sierra cups to clients to tie to their belts so they could drink from the river. This was a new experience for most of them. To drink directly from a stream would be suicidal where they came from. By 1980, the Sierra cup was no longer hanging from belts, following a number of emergency flights into the Middle Fork backcountry strips to fly out victims of Giardiasis.

On a ski trip in the White Clouds in 1980, we chopped a hole in the ice on the creek to fill a canteen. I should have known better, but was not thinking *Giardia*. Beaver still poop in the water under the ice. Seven days later, John was passed out and enroute to the hospital where he spent the next twenty-four hours on IVs to rebuild his fluids. Although my daughter Judi and I drank from the same canteen, neither of us were infected. After that, I was extremely cautious about my water consumption. It had to be filtered under seven micron size or brought to a boil. *Giardia* cysts are killed at 176 degrees F.

I was on a helicopter survey counting mountain goats in the Frank Church Wilderness one spring, staying at the Taylor Ranch on lower Big Creek. I was unaware that the outfitter was making the orange juice for breakfast with raw creek water. Five days after I got out, I was again bathroom bound. *Giardia* got me one more time while kayaking the Boise River. The most effective treatment for us has been a ten day dosage of Flagyl, which for some folks is a double whammy, since you get violently ill if you drink any alcohol.

For thirty years I had consumed mountain waters with impunity, and suddenly even wilderness streams were unfit. I always maintained that water was a lousy drink. Within a few years, Giardiasis was epidemic. I suspect that it was always present in animal populations, but at very low levels and probably cycled out of local areas within a couple generations. It is known that a percentage of the human population is infected with *Giardia*, without showing symptoms. My theory is that these individuals were healthy enough to access the backcountry and were the primary carriers of the parasite, reinfecting wild animal populations through poor sanitary habits. Beavers are not the culprits, we are.

12 | Winter Secrets

EVERY TIME I MADE A TRIP on my Army surplus snowshoes, I felt I was being punished for something I had done, but didn't know what it was. If the new hi-tech snowshoes available now had come out in 1974, I may have stayed with that mode of snow travel, but instead I became deeply hooked on cross-country skiing. Nearly every weekend I would ski up to Deer Point and then east on the ridge along the Boise Front.

One winter, I realized I could get in a lot more skiing if I stayed overnight on the ridge. I had never built a snow cave for winter camping. There were some big drifts on the ridge that could be easily dug into, and the snow cave was a complete success. I slept warmer than in fall hunting camps. A candle and trapped body heat kept the cave temperature near forty degrees. I had discovered the secret. Don't camp on top of the snow, camp underneath it.

I learned how to compact snow, cut out building blocks with a snow saw, and construct a snow trench and the traditional igloo. These snow shelters afforded greater winter camping options. Soon our kids were involved with cross-country skiing and winter camping trips in the mountains. The longer trips were usually during spring break when school was out. Following is the journal of one trip we took in 1980 into the White Clouds:

White Clouds Diary, March 23, 1980

We stayed overnight at Joe Leonard's Lodge at Stanley. They have a great cook there by the name of Sandy (last name Gebhards). She fed us each what had to be a 3-pound omelet with trimmings for breakfast. Unfortunately, she had to work all week, so John, Judi, and I headed for the East Fork of the Salmon without her. Always hate to leave a good cook behind. It had been ten years since I was up Little Boulder Creek trail by horse, and it took a little while to figure where the trailhead was for sure. We got started around 1230 and climbed nearly an hour before we could put skis on. Saw several herds of deer, 15 to 20 to a bunch.

By 1600 we were pretty well burned out and had covered only 3 1/2 miles. The packs are heavy, 60 and 70 pounds, and we are badly out of shape. We made a tarp shelter in an aspen grove for our evening camp. The snow is only two feet deep and too sugary to make into blocks.

March 24. Temperature 14 degrees F. The packs are still just as heavy as yesterday. Name of the game today is one foot in front of the other. Passed Red Ridge and got to the big meadow below Castle Peak around 1500. We camped on a knoll overlooking the meadow with Castle Peak and Serrate Ridge for a backdrop. Set up another tarp shelter and built a snow trench.

March 25. I almost overslept. The sun was just hitting Castle Peak, the timbered valley below was still black. I had to have this picture, raced out of the snow trench in my stocking feet, snow to my knees, camera in hand. I got one of the most striking photos I've ever taken. Temperature, 0 degrees. We had buttermilk pancakes and maple syrup for breakfast with a great view from the kitchen. I don't think we had really made up our minds which route to take until we heard avalanches cracking like cannon fire up Slickenside Canyon. Then we knew for certain we wanted to head up to Boulder Chain Lakes.

We had nearly made it to the second lake when John's left boot would no longer stay in the binding. I was able to tie it in with nylon cord. Arrived at the north side of the lake at 1500, elevation 8,900 feet. Weather was clear and I skied the entire day in my T-shirt, even though it was zero in the morning. We tramped out snow, let it set for an hour, and started cutting snow blocks. Judi made a snow trench, John and I had an igloo up in 1 1/2 hours. Beautiful campsite with a backdrop across the lake and a huge rock pinnacle.

March 26. I was a little concerned about the meals the other morning when I saw the kids popping vitamin pills. Didn't think the food was too bad until dinner last night, which was a package of Dri-Lite: Spaghetti and Meatballs #4076. According to the label, "Italian alpine packers would love this dish if they could lay their hands on it. (If they did, they'd declare war on America again.) It's one of the heartiest meals you can fix on the trail." Well, I don't know about the "hearty," but it was one of the thickest meals I ever cooked. John thought it was some kind of red epoxy and was going to repair the toe of his boot with it.

Temperature 2 degrees, shelter temperatures over 30 degrees. Weather started out clear, sunshine and everyone seemed to have survived #4076. By noon it had clouded up and started to snow, but we decided to explore the Boulder Chain Lakes anyway. We skied to the upper lake, elevation 9,415, snow and fog limit any picture taking. Took three hours of climbing from camp, and one hour to ski back. Still snowing hard as we sat out on the patio in front of the igloo, John reading a book and Judi sewing up a hole in her gloves. Before supper I decided to check out a big open slope on the ridge across the lake. It was a north face and superb powder on a 25 degree slope. I reported back at camp, and within 20 minutes the kids were on it. After supper they went back again wearing headlamps, while I watched their lights weaving down the mountainside.

Later that night, Judi and I climbed up to the ridge. The moon appeared out of the high mist, and we could see the White Cloud peaks swathed in the cold, moonlit stillness. Below us lay a wilderness panorama, broken only by the flicker of the candle lantern across the lake at camp.

March 27. Discovered I lost all the maps yesterday on our tour. Oh well, Joe lost his compass up here on his last trip, so at least there's a matched set here someplace. Got up at 0630 and had planned to climb the mountain south of the lake, but we had a blizzard in progress. Crawled back into the igloo, checked again at 0900, still snowing hard. I set up a tarp to cook under, skied the powder slope some more, then took the rest of the day off and read a book.

March 28. Clear skies, temperature 2 degrees, no wind. We voted to climb the ridge across from camp and up the mountain as far as we could get by noon, then ski down. It took an hour to get to the top of the ridge. We could see all the way to the Big Lost River range and Mount Borah, Idaho's highest peak, over 12,000 feet elevation.

As we came over the crest of the ridge, I knew the mountain was going to be there, but was still unprepared for the view. Suddenly, there loomed Castle Peak like a giant cathedral, dusted with powder from the storm. I fully expected to hear organ music coming from it. We skied virgin powder snow for an hour and then, reluctantly, dropped back down to camp. Packed up and skied to the lower campsite on Little Boulder Creek meadows.

March 29. Breakfast menu, hash brown potatoes and beef patties. Didn't get our gear packed up until 1100, but the late start was of no matter, since we skied the eight miles out in four hours. We stopped at Sullivan Hot Springs on the way back to see what hot water felt like again.

After seven days of living in the snow, eating snow, cooking with snow water, what was the first thing the kids bought at the general store in Clayton? Yep, ice cream bars.

Cold Survival Basics

Our lifetime experiences have shaped our survival instincts. We think we know what is absolutely essential: fire, food, water, clothing, and insulated shelter. How do we provide for these basic elements in an emergency situation, and are they all necessary? Cold survival is the prevention of heat loss from the body and is accomplished by:

1. Conserving energy—no unnecessary exertion.

2. Wearing clothing or fabrics that insulate when wet.

3. Finding/building a protective shelter that insulates.

4. Preventing body contact with cold surfaces.

Fire

We live in the mountains of central Idaho, and my first chore on a winter morning is to start the wood stove. Fire has come to symbolize cold survival, so much so, that nearly every survival manual goes into great detail on fire building in the snow, often listing it as first priority. In other words, you are going to die without it. This is a fallacy that has been embellished by fiction writers, television, and movies.

Over the past forty-five years, I have worked and played in the Rocky Mountains during winter, involving week-long trips on skis, snow camps over 9,400 feet elevation, temperatures down to minus thirty-five degrees F, and countless blizzards. During all that time, I built only one wood fire. It was in the Sawtooth Mountains in 1979 when my backpack stove quit working and I wanted to boil water for coffee.

Doing without a fire for warmth and survival seems illogical, especially at sub-zero temperatures. Consider this: you will need to gather a supply of dry wood that will provide enough heat for twelve hours, assuming only one night out on the mountain. Finding dry wood can be a challenge, if at all possible, and collecting it another, unless you pack around a saw or axe. Without such tools, a three-inch diameter limb is about the largest a person can break off. Collecting wood requires a great deal of energy, working up a good sweat. These are two body conditions that should be avoided when faced with a cold weather emergency. Depleted energy reserves and damp clothing can be a fatal combination. A shovel will be necessary to dig down to ground level, otherwise the fire begins to sink out of sight as soon as it is lit. Of course, a fire platform can be made from green logs as shown in some manuals, but not many winter recreationists carry around an axe and a chainsaw.

Food and Water

With cellular phones, portable radios, GPS units, snowmobiles with backcountry capability, aircraft, and all the high-tech equipment that exists today, search and rescue efforts are usually successful within twenty-four hours to a few days. No one is going to starve within that time period. A person can exist without food for several weeks. Dehydration can be of concern if expending a lot of energy. If water is not available, eat snow. This will not seriously drain your heat reserve; just make sure it's the right color.

Clothing

Your survival kit is the clothing you put on before you go out the door or leave camp. Cotton fabric shirts or trousers are the worst choice for snow conditions. When cotton gets damp or soaking wet, it stays that way for a long time, loses insulating quality, and accelerates body heat loss. Wool has been a winter favorite for centuries, resists water, insulates when wet, and lasts for many seasons of hard wear. The modern polyester fabrics, originally called polypropylene, and fleece garments, sold under a variety of trade names, are truly amazing. These have the unique property of rapid drying from body heat alone, reject moisture, and will insulate when soaking wet. I have worked for hours in the snow with wet, polyester gloves and still had warm hands. I have also had wool mittens freeze solid on the outside with my hands warm inside.

An ideal survival kit would be long underwear, socks, shirt, trousers, gloves or mittens, cap with ear flaps, all made from polyester or wool, and an outer shell of windproof/water resistant hooded parka and over-pants. With this kit, a person can survive a long time with little else.

Insulated Shelter

With the exception of goose down, snow may be one of nature's most efficient insulating materials. Snow contains 50 to 80 percent air space which performs the same function as in artificial insulators like clothing, fiberglass, or Styrofoam. Yet, most people consider sleeping in the snow a terminal experience. Each winter we read sad accounts of victims who chose to stay inside a familiar surrounding that represents safety and shelter, such as a stalled vehicle or abandoned cabin. Without insulation and supplemental heat, these are no better at sub-zero temperatures than sleeping inside a chest freezer.

Some years ago, an Idaho pilot and two passengers made a successful crash landing in the winter in the mountains of northern Utah. Injuries were minor, their location was determined, and a rescue party reached them the next day. The plane seemed the secure place to stay inside for the night. Temperatures dropped to minus thirty degrees F and they were found frozen to death by the rescuers. These people had spent their last hours looking out of windows of the plane at the very thing that could have saved them, snow. I have slept overnight in a snow shelter with only six inches of compacted snow for insulation at thirty degrees below zero and was able to maintain a temperature advantage of fifty degrees warmer from my body heat trapped inside the shelter.

On Mores Mountain, elevation 6,980 feet, on December 15, 1984 I turned on my flashlight to see what time it was: 6:45 a.m. The thermometer inside the shelter read thirty-two degrees F, as I had expected it would. I felt chilled, but I wasn't shivering. I could tell time and temperature—my mind seemed clear. Although it had been a long, cold night with only intermittent sleep, I was not hypothermic—the experimental shelter worked.

I pushed through the fir boughs covering the entry and a cold, sharp wind filled with needle-like crystals of snow greeted me as I emerged. Outside air temperature was fourteen degrees F with a chill factor calculated at minus ten degrees. My previously untested shelter concept had provided a temperature advantage of forty-two degrees. It had kept me alive and without any cold-related injury overnight. Nor did I have a fire or sleeping bag. Not bad for something constructed in forty-five minutes.

The day before, I had snowshoed up the mountain to a timbered area to field test a shelter design I had worked out on paper. I wanted to simulate a worst-case situation of a person caught overnight in the mountains in winter with only what they were wearing. I informed my daughter about my plans and where I would be. Always inform someone where you are going and when you expect to return. I did not explain the full details to my wife, as I knew she would have had me committed before I got out of town, or, she would have taken out more insurance on me.

So how did I manage to sleep in the snow overnight on a mountain top without a sleeping bag at ten degrees below zero?

- I picked a heavily wooded area with accessible fir boughs I could break off. My shelter took less than an hour to construct and required little energy.

- I was wearing polypropylene underwear, shirt, and jacket; wool socks, pants, and mittens, all of which absorb little water and still retain insulation. This type of shelter did not involve body contact with the snow, as with the construction of a snow cave, so only my gloves got wet. I had a warm cap with ear flaps and an extra pair of dry gloves for bedtime, which were important because a major amount of radiated heat is lost through uncovered hands and head. I was wearing my survival kit.

- The six or more inches of snow on the roof of the fir boughs trapped heat inside and kept cold out. When snow depths exceed three feet, the temperature of the snow at ground level is thirty-two degrees. If the floor of the shelter is near ground level, this exposes a natural "earth furnace" that can be forty to sixty degrees warmer than the surface snow. Additional heat radiated from your body and from respiration adds to the warming of the shelter.

- A thick layer of boughs on the floor and sides of the trench, and over me as a blanket, kept me from direct contact with the snow.

Constructing the emergency shelter

- Select an area that has lots of trees close by with low-hanging limbs. Fir is the best building material. These are the ones with the short, flat needles, but any evergreen will work. I would avoid the sharp-needled spruce, since this would be like sleeping on porcupines.

- Limbs up to an inch in diameter or more can be easily snapped off by hand. They should be at least four feet in length for the roof support. Shorter pieces can be used for the trench floor and lining the sides.

- Use snowshoes, skis, or feet to create a trench in the snow three feet wide, thirty inches deep, and two feet longer than your body length. Of course, a backpack shovel works even better.

- Push the butt ends of the four-foot limbs into the top edge of the trench to form an A-frame or peaked roof. The ends of the limbs from either side must overlap at the peak.

- As the roof is being constructed, start filling in the floor with a thick layer of boughs. Fir boughs have a natural curve to them and if placed the right way, can give additional spring to the mattress. Sides are lined by jamming butt ends into the floor. Snow that falls onto the floor boughs will filter on through by shaking.

- When the roof is complete, cover it with at least six inches of snow; twelve inches will be more than adequate. The boughs will support some 200 pounds of snow on the roof.

- Cover the entry with boughs and snow, leaving just enough space to crawl through. Once inside, seal the entry with more boughs and your pack if you have one. It may be a long, cold night, but you will be able to see the sunrise in the morning.

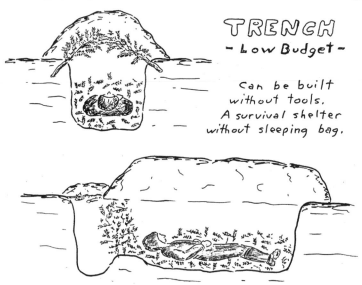

TRENCH
– Low Budget –

Can be built
without tools.
A survival shelter
without sleeping bag.

Interior temperatures of snow caves or trenches will not drop below thirty-two degrees and generally range up to thirty-eight degrees without any additional heat sources. One or two candles left burning will elevate the temperature to forty-four degrees in a small shelter. Larger snow shelters, such as a three-person igloo, are not as heat efficient but will still not drop below thirty degrees. Ventilation usually is not a problem unless the interior walls become excessively iced over and the entry is tightly sealed. If it becomes stuffy inside, simply poke a hole in the roof or open the entry. Cooking inside a snow shelter can be dangerous. Carbon monoxide is given off by a backpack stove or gas lantern. Since it is 3 percent lighter than air, it can be vented with a hole in the roof if it is necessary to cook inside. Heat from a camp stove will quickly raise the interior temperature to over seventy degrees, so the number of meals cooked inside is obviously limited and can create some troublesome dripping.

Another safety consideration is the location of the shelter. Is it in a potential avalanche track or runout zone? Do not use a tree well around the base of a tree as a campsite during a heavy snowstorm or if snow accumulations are evident on the tree. Snow shelters or tents will not survive several hundred pounds of snow falling twenty or thirty feet onto the roof.

Minimal Equipment

Volumes have been written on the items that should be in a survival kit. What you carry should be tailored to the season and type of trip. When I was ski guiding, I carried much more than when alone, so I could respond to any needs of the group. If you attempt to cover too many probabilities, the kit will soon be too heavy to carry. I have seen some that weighed over forty pounds and contained everything but a flush toilet. There is a big difference between survival items and things that only make you more comfortable. Over the years, your kit will shrink as you eliminate things that are never used. This is how mine looks after forty-five years of trimming, and these items are applicable for all seasons. Included in my pack or saddle bags are:

- Nylon tarp, 10' x 12', for protection in wind, rain, snow

- Nylon rope for the tarp, lashing poles, repairs

- Plastic trash bag, black, large size. Use as emergency poncho or ground cloth. On a sunny day, the bag laid flat will act as a solar heat attractor. Snow sprinkled lightly on the bag will melt and collect in the depressions. I have collected 3 1/2 cups of water this way in forty-five minutes.

- Swiss Army knife

- Pocket flashlight and extra batteries

- Compass

- Extra pair of polyester gloves and stocking cap

- Minor repair items: duct tape, nylon straps, leather laces

- Backpack shovel, winter only

- Matches carried in 35mm film canister, pitchwood firestarter, candles

- First aid: stretch fabric knuckle band-aids, moleskin, Telfa pads, elastic cling bandage roll, Tylenol, salt tablets for muscle cramps.

Snow Snakes

The snow snake is a nonpoisonous creature, rarely seen during winter. In the summer they seem to melt away until the next snowfall. Get bit by one, and it's like being on drugs, you always have this craving for snow. All the kids have been bitten, but I think Sandy suffered the most extreme reaction from a bite. One day in February 1979, she came to me and said she was going on a 200-mile ski expedition for three weeks, starting at Grangeville, through the Gospel-Hump Wilderness, across the Salmon River up to Chamberlain Basin, down Big Creek, back up Monumental Creek to the mining town of Yellowpine. She would join a group of eight skiers, including one other woman.

On the fourth day of the trip, Sandy had slipped, fallen backwards, and was sliding helplessly on her pack, head first down an avalanche chute. She slid for 100 feet, coming to a stop in some boulders at the edge of a cliff, relatively unhurt. Eight days later, Sandy and her companions skied into the old town of Dixie, behind schedule and out of food, having been hit daily with heavy snow storms, and whiteouts, and climbing through avalanche paths filled with snow blocks and broken trees.

Five of the group pulled out at Dixie, including Sandy's female companion who had injured her neck. Resupplied, the remaining three headed down into the Salmon River Canyon to Campbells Ferry, homestead of Frances Wisner. Frances was said to be sometimes intolerant of strangers, especially men. The male segment of the group was glad to have Sandy along as peace envoy. She and Frances became instant friends and the boys had a place to sleep that night.

Too far behind the trip schedule, with school and work commitments pulling at them, they decided to fly out. Campbells Ferry was the halfway point and the last place they could get out from before Yellowpine. Ron Watters, who had been the originator of the expedition, continued on solo, completing the original route plan, and arrived in Yellowpine eight days later. Ron published one of the better books on ski camping, utilizing photos and experience gained during Sandy's ski adventure. She could write her own book on gourmet camp cooking and wilderness encounters, such as fending off a bunch of drunken Texas elk hunters with a butcher knife in the kitchen of the Stonebraker Ranch and escaping into the woods at night, or being pinned on a raft in Tappan Falls on the Middle Fork of the Salmon.

Snow School

The Idaho Outfitters and Guides Board required that a person pass a three-day winter field exam in the mountains before receiving a ski-guide license. Our exam took place in the Sawtooths, skiing in to Hell Roaring and Imogene lakes. One of the test exercises was to start a warming fire within five minutes. All had a fire going except one fellow who could not get his started. In desperation, he poured white gas on his wood pile when no one was looking. He touched a match to it just as the examiner came up to see how he was doing. I don't think he scored too well on the exercise, as his warming fire was soon scattered all over a thirty-foot area. I fared a little better, passed the exam, and was licensed in 1979 as a lead guide for backcountry skiing with Leonard Expeditions in Stanley. Joe Leonard was the first in Idaho and perhaps the United States to initiate the European custom of touring to ski huts. His original huts were canvas wall tents, with bunks and wood stoves. The tents were later replaced with the Mongolian yurts.

Bob Sevy, another Sawtooth ski outfitter, Joe, Sandy and I had skied up to Alpine Lake on Iron Creek. It was late March, and end of the winter tourist season. Bob and Joe wanted to relax and celebrate, away from the hassles of guiding and waiting on strangers. The weather had been mild, so we elected to bring two backpack tents in lieu of building snow shelters. After a supper of steak, potatoes, and green beans, Joe produced a bottle of whiskey from his tent. This went down on top of the dandelion wine that we had with supper. Soon the whiskey was gone and Bob said, "What'll we do now? It's too early to go to bed." I reached into my pack and pulled out a plastic water bottle filled with moonshine medicine.

We decided to have a contest. The last person still on his feet was the winner and got to drink whatever was left. Sandy had already dropped out of the competition and gone to our tent. Neither Bob nor Joe noticed in the darkness that I had taken my ski pole, shoved the handle under my belt buckle, and leaned into it. My body from the waist down was a tripod, and no way could I fall over. Once we had taken all of our medicine, Bob and Joe's legs turned to mush. They conceded victory and fell over backwards into their tent.

When I removed the ski pole, I recognized immediately that I had a problem. Our tent was fifty feet away and was moving. I chased it through the snow around camp for about fifteen minutes before I was able to grab it as it passed by. Sandy was kind enough to stuff me down into my sleeping bag, although it would have taken a long time to freeze anything with that much alcohol in it.

The sun was obscenely bright when it hit the door of the tent. I unzipped the fly, stuck my head out, and was greeted at the entry with my supper lying there in the snow. It was almost pretty, with the sun backlighting the feathery hoarfrost crystals that covered the green beans.

The Tripod Position has since been disqualified at drinking contests in the Sawtooths.

My winter excursions provided an extensive reference source of 35mm color slides. These I used for the development of a lecture series on snow shelters, equipment, winter first aid, ski techniques, and avalanche awareness. The program, called Idaho Snow School, also included an overnight camp in the mountains where students built and slept in their own snow shelters. Initially it was taught through Boise City Recreation and Boise State University's Outdoor Adventure Program. Sandy and John had become experts in winter mountaineering and skiing, and I utilized them, whenever I could, as assistant instructors. I gave the winter mountaineering training to Idaho Fish and Game personnel, U.S. Forest Service, Idaho Department of Transportation, Idaho Mountain Search and Rescue, leaders of the Boy Scouts and Girl Scouts of America, conservation officers in British Columbia, an instructor cadre for the U.S. Army Special Forces, and Bureau of Land Management radio technicians who service the remote area weather stations (RAWS) nationwide.

Bob McCormick supervised the RAWS group out of Boise and hired me to do their winter training for several years. On one trip to Pilot Peak, north of Idaho City, they rolled a snow machine on me and broke my leg. It was the fibula and I thought it was just a sprained ankle. Sandy had come along as an assistant so I had her supervise the snow shelter building, since I wasn't getting around too well. That night in my snow trench, I realized it was more than a sprain and consumed all the aspirins I could find in my first aid kit.

I returned to Boise the next day and took off my ski boot for the first time since the accident. It did not look good and Maria hauled me off to the emergency room at St. Lukes Hospital. The ER nurse was filling out the accident form and asked if I had iced my ankle down after the injury. I replied, "No, but I slept in a snow trench with that leg outside my sleeping bag, does that count?" Then she asked if I had kept it elevated. I answered, "Well, I was at 8,000 feet and I couldn't go any higher." Some nurses have no sense of humor at all.

Too Close for Comfort

The last big snow training exercise was in eastern Idaho for a county sheriff's search and rescue team in 1993. Al Nicholson, regional conservation officer for Fish and Game in Region Six, asked if he and some Fish and Game personnel could hook up with us for an extra day. I told the county deputy to select a site that had three or more feet of snow and would be within a mile or so of the trailhead. There were twenty people scheduled to go and for safety reasons, I did not want to get very far out. John agreed to come along and help out as an instructor.

Transportation to the camp was a fleet of snowmobiles with the county search team in the lead. This was completely new country to me. We crossed over several miles of dry farm bench land and dropped into a canyon that went up into the Targhee Forest. We had gone way beyond what I had requested for a camp site and I told the deputy, this is as far as we go. I suspect what they had done was gone into their favorite snowmachine playground, so they would have ready-built snow shelters to use later on during the winter. I had an uneasy feeling about our location and the distance from our departure point.

The county group went out the following day, as Fish and Game came in. That night it began to snow. By noon, when we broke camp the next day, there was a foot of new snow and more falling. Bob McCormick had come over from Boise to help John and me with instructing the first two days, then went out with the county. He told me later that the entire Upper Snake River Valley was filled with lenticular clouds. Had I known that, we would have left camp the next day at first light. We were down in a canyon, in heavy timber, and unable to observe the cloud formations.

The new snow made tough going for the snowmachines that were pulling cargo sleds, even on a flat trail down the canyon. We had a struggle getting the machines 300 yards up the hillside to the bench lands. This took about an hour, punching out a trail, little by little. On top, the storm took on a completely different character with fierce winds. The snow falling was now horizontal instead of vertical, and visibility was reduced to thirty yards.

We tightened up the group to maintain visual contact, stopping occasionally to count machines and riders. It was on one of these stops that I realized something had changed. The cargo sleds were gone! They had left them back down in the canyon so they could get the machines up the hill. On the sleds were their packs, snowshoes, shovels, everything except the clothes they were wearing.

The only equipment we had was on my toboggan that was built from four old cross-country skis. It could carry over 100 pounds, was no wider than a snowmachine track, and did not create the drag of a big cargo sled. John and I had our packs, but I knew we could not adequately take care of ten people with what we had. I was riding with John on one machine with the toboggan. We were following the lead snowmachine, snow was blowing horizontally from our left, then gradually changed and was blowing from our right. John pulled up alongside the leader and got him stopped. He had traveled in a complete circle.

One of the snowmachines ran out of gas. The extra gas was back down in the canyon on the abandoned cargo sleds. The remaining snowmachines were perilously low on fuel and returning to the sleds was no longer an option. Barren of any trees, the high and dry farm benchlands were exposed to the fury of the winds and the blowing snow that was whipped to near whiteout conditions. No landmarks were visible and we realized that within another thirty minutes our situation would deteriorate rapidly—darkness was approaching, the snowmachines would be out of gas, and effective shelter in the high winds and blowing snow was questionable. We had to get back to the ranch house where we originally departed.

There have been times in the mountains when I had to rely upon the homing instincts of the horse or mule I was riding to take me safely through the darkness and storm at night back to camp. John seemed to have those same intuitive navigational skills and I felt more at ease when he took over as lead snowmachine. I was not surprised, then, when twenty minutes later, we were following the power poles to the ranch.

Avalanche

I hadn't planned to do a section on snow avalanches until a couple events occurred during the winter of 1997. John lost a friend of his in an avalanche in northern Utah in January and a snowmobiler was killed thirty miles from our home. The accident in Utah killed three snow campers and was a matter of bad timing. The one here in Valley County was a matter of stupidity. The fact that more people are not killed in avalanches is simply a function of dumb luck. There are certain snow conditions that will place you at high risk and if you ignore those conditions on a regular basis, the process of natural selection will remove you from the population. This is called survival of the informed.

The group that John's friend was in consisted of experienced, cautious backcountry skiers. They had taken advanced precautions of calling avalanche forecasting services prior to their trip and were advised that the area they planned to tour should be safe. Avalanche frequency at a given location may occur after each major storm, or can be similar to flood frequencies, happening every five, twenty-five, or one hundred years, depending upon weather conditions. The Utah avalanche that caught the three at night in their tent was a once in 300 years event.

The Valley County snowmobiler was found twenty-four hours later, buried under three feet of snow, and located with probe poles. The fact that he was not wearing a transceiver indicates that he and his two associates had no training or knowledge in avalanche safety or awareness. A transceiver is a battery operated unit that is worn by a skier/snowmobiler and transmits a signal which can be picked up by a similar unit when switched to the receive mode. A person buried in an avalanche can be located in ten minutes or less. This is a critical time period, since two-thirds of the victims die of suffocation. Locating is one thing, removal of the victim in time is another. If there are no shovels in the party, there will not be a rescue. Avalanche debris is under such pressures that even powder snow will bond within minutes and set up like concrete.

If you are buried in an avalanche, there's a 70 percent chance you will end up as a statistic. Survival rates for the first twenty minutes are about 80 percent; 40 percent after one hour; and very poor beyond two hours because an ice mask will form over the face, sealing off oxygen that would normally filter through the snow. Survival rates are only 45 percent when buried no deeper than eighteen inches; 1 percent if buried at six feet; and zip at nine feet or deeper. When you consider the tremendous forces of an avalanche, you can understand why one-third of the fatalities are related to physical injuries.

The three snowmobilers were using specially modified machines which have the capability of traveling the extreme elevation backcountry terrain. They were playing a game, called highmarking, to see who could go up the highest and on the steepest slopes. The group had made several runs up the slope until the victim made it to the top underneath an overhanging snow cornice, and triggered the avalanche (most are set off by the victim). Any good reference book on avalanches will list the highest hazard as a slope immediately below a large cornice. This is an area that receives heavy deposition of wind-blown snow over a ridge and builds up into a very unstable slab, sometimes within a few hours. The weight of a single skier can set off one of these slabs, let alone a 500 to 600 pound snowmachine and 200 pound rider. This would have the same effect as lobbing an artillery shell onto the slope. The Russians play a game similar to this, except instead of using a snowmachine, they use a revolver.

Avalanche releases are a highly complex event involving a number of variables, some of which may change within an hour's time. Major factors that affect the development of avalanche conditions and their release are slope angle, slope aspect, ground cover, altitude, snow crystal type, snowfall intensity, depth of snowpack, temperatures within the snowpack, snow metamorphosis, ground radiation, wind velocity, wind direction, rain, and storm frequency.

Most avalanches occur on slopes between thirty and forty-five degrees, with the highest frequency at thirty-five to forty degrees. North aspect slopes tend to be less stable in early winter, more stable in spring; south slopes are more stable in early winter, less stable in spring because of solar heating. Wind-scoured slopes are generally safer due to compaction and reduced snow depth. Leeward slopes can receive major deposits of transported snow when winds exceed fifteen miles per hour. Vertical, treeless pathways down a mountainside are likely avalanche paths. Reference books, videos, and field training seminars are available. These resources, along with good judgment, can keep you out of the obituary page.

Snow trench camp at Imogene Lake in the Sawtooth National Recreation Area, March 1979. *Stacy Gebhards photo.*

13 | The Lenticulars are Coming

FAILURE TO BE ABLE TO FORECAST changes in mountain weather can range from mere inconvenience to a survival situation. In September 1985, Wes and I were moose hunting along the west slope of the Tetons in Wyoming. That morning we had observed lenticular clouds moving through the valley, accentuating what was otherwise a clear, warm day. We knew from experience that lenticulars can precede violent cold fronts by four to twenty-four hours, so we added foul weather gear and warm clothing to our saddle packs. At 4:00 that afternoon we were at 9,000 feet elevation when the storm hit, bringing eighty mile an hour winds and wet, driving snow—a deadly combination for the unprepared.

Not ten miles from our location, five mountain climbers on the Grand Teton were in serious trouble. They had left camp that morning confident that the clear weather would hold for an ascent of the 13,766 foot peak. Only one person had taken the routine precaution of carrying extra clothing, foul weather gear, food, and water, standard items for the prevention of hypothermia. The blizzard took quick toll of the unprepared and three died on the mountain. The other two were near death when rescued by the heroic efforts of National Park Service rangers. This tragedy might have been avoided had the climbers been adequately equipped or aware of the message being sent that morning by those long funny-looking, cigar-shaped clouds. Lenticular clouds are singular. Sometimes you see only two or three drifting through. On a clear day, the upper half will look silvery with a dark underside.

If you examine the case history of any winter injury, accident, or emergency, you will find that at some point, poor judgment was involved. In most instances, bad weather is a key player.

Mt. Hood, Oregon, May 12, 1986: eight college students and their group leader died of hypothermia on the mountain and the sole survivor suffered the amputation of both legs. Although the leader had made eighteen such trips on Mt. Hood, this expedition was a litany of bad judgment. The climbers lacked basic equipment, protective clothing, and decided to press on to the summit in a fierce blizzard. I had been on the Oregon coast the day before and recall hearing the weather forecasts of a large, severe storm that would hit the coastline on May 12.

No matter that you have the latest in equipment, hi-tech clothing, survival gear, communications, and years of training and experience: use poor judgment and you can have a very bad day.

Weather Forecasting

For over twenty-five years I carried a compass with me in the Selway Wilderness. Only once was I ever able to shoot two bearings on geographical features and accurately fix a position on a map. Not to imply that I was lost the rest of the time: you are in thick timber, down in a canyon, or the weather precludes seeing further than the opposite hillside. An altimeter, however, allows you to pinpoint your location on a USGS contour map with greater precision than your best compass triangulation. You can do it in any weather condition, day or night.

In addition to the navigational advantages of an altimeter, you can also achieve a high degree of accuracy in short-term—twenty-four to forty-eight hours—weather forecasting. That alone can save you a lot of time, agony, and expense when you are in the mountains. The altimeter responds to changes in elevation and atmospheric pressure. At a fixed elevation in camp, it will function as a barometer. A falling barometer heralds the arrival of a low pressure system and associated storms. As you climb in elevation, air pressure decreases, and the altimeter registers an increase in height. An atmospheric low pressure system will cause an altimeter at a fixed location to show an increasing elevation without being moved. So, a rising altimeter is synonymous with a falling barometer. Conversely, a falling altimeter indicates high pressure and improving weather.

If you wake up in the morning and find that your camp elevation is 300 or 400 feet higher than at bedtime, make sure the slickers are tied on behind the saddles. A change of 100 feet elevation up to 10,000 feet is equivalent to 0.10 inches mercury on the barometer. A rapid change—50 to 100 feet in three hours or less—generally forecasts rapidly changing weather that may last only one or two days. Slow changes are associated with longer-lasting weather conditions, whether stormy or clearing.

Cold fronts move rapidly: up to 500 to 700 miles in a day. These may arrive with little advance warning, often within a few hours. A reliable predictor in the Intermountain West is the presence of lenticular clouds. Although these storms may be of short duration, they are generally more violent than those produced by a warm front. The actual cold front may be preceded by a squall line 50 to 200 miles in advance.

Warm fronts move more slowly, 250 to 500 miles a day, producing lower cloud ceilings, poor visibility, and precipitation lasting several days. They may be preceded up to forty-eight hours by high altitude cirrus clouds, also called mares' tails, and a slow drop in barometric pressure. Don't expect to become a meteorologist with an altimeter and watching clouds, but an awareness of what might be coming your way could be of vital interest on the mountain.

Wes Rose, the author's hunting partner of more than forty years, packing in on the Upper Selway River, Selway/Bitterroot Wilderness. *Stacy Gebhards photo.*

14 | Saddles and Sores

I F MOST OF YOUR RIDING experience has been limited to bridle paths, flat land, or an occasional weekend deer hunt in the fall, there are a few things you ought to know about the use of horses and mules in the mountains.

Smokey

If you lived in Salmon in the 1950s and traveled the backcountry, you had to have a horse. I could only scrape together $75 and found a cowboy that would sell me a bay mare at that price. He said I was getting a heck of a deal, two for one, since she'd been bred by a big black mustang out on the range up by Leadore. Sure enough, on July 1, 1958, I went out to the pasture and there was the prettiest colt you ever saw. Long legs, black mane and tail, white star, and the color of blue smoke. He turned out to be the best mountain horse I ever worked with.

I needed a good saddle and liked the style of Clyde Johnston, a saddle maker who lived at Meyers Cove on Camas Creek. Clyde was caretaker at the old fluorospar mine, trapped beaver, guided sheep hunters, and built saddles when he was snowed in for the winter. He had been a cowboy and bronc rider in Utah when he was younger, and claimed his mother had been one of the child survivors of the Mountain Meadows Massacre in southern Utah. I've since put forty years and around 12,000 miles of riding in the mountains on that saddle.

Well, nothing is perfect, and neither was Smokey. Although I could shoe horses, I figured it would be best if I had a professional do his first set. With a good first experience at being shod, my life would be a whole lot easier in the future. The local farrier in Jerome, where I was now stationed as area fisheries biologist, was built like a Dallas Cowboys linebacker. This should have been a piece of cake. After considerable difficulty on the front end, he finally got to the first hind leg. Quickly, a cloud of dust developed, followed by a thud, and a loud groan. When the dust settled, I could see the farrier holding his side, shirt ripped from the tail to his collar, and the buttons blown off the suspenders of his bib overalls that were now down around his ankles. Looking at this huge, sweaty man standing there in the corral in his underwear, I sensed that my hopes for a pleasant experience for all concerned might be in question.

In the years that followed, Smokey's reputation somehow preceded him. Local farriers always seemed to have a full schedule, especially the ones that wore bib overalls. I suffered through years of dust clouds, broken halter ropes, and busted fence posts, and acquired a few scars from horseshoe nails. And, all my kids, while helping me, learned first hand how to speak mule skinners' English.

Most folks think that shoeing horses and mules, breaking them to ride and pack, requires an extensive four-letter vocabulary. Not so. All you need is the Universal Command, which is a twenty-four-letter word: Goddamyousonofabitchwhoa. With a little practice this command will roll off your tongue like the crack of a whip and is applicable in all situations of chaos, panic, and total destruction. Beyond that, you can then resort to the conventional four-letter vocabulary.

Smokey more than compensated for his character flaw when he was in the mountains. He could go places where I couldn't even stand up. I'm sure he inherited the Wild Thing from his mustang daddy. We packed a lot of fish into mountain lakes that had no trails to them. I would come back a couple years later to restock the lake. Smokey would step off the trail and head for the lake without my touching the reins. His sense of direction was better than a Global Positioning System unit—a system that uses triangulation with orbiting satellites to affix the position of the transmitting unit. I always let Smokey make the final decision on how to get back to camp.

It was the last day of elk season. I had offered to help locate elk for some friends of mine from Jerome, Doc Sloat and Wes and Mary Rose. I had seen elk earlier in the summer while packing fish on the upper South Fork of the Boise River. We rode the horses up through a narrow gap on the ridge and dropped down into Bass Lakes below Two-Point Mountain. Doc shot an elk just before dark. We finished quartering and hanging the meat by flashlight, planning to come back the next day and pack it out.

Lightning and thunder had forewarned us of a big storm coming and it hit us with a vengeance. Torrential rain soon turned into a wet, heavy snow. I had to find the gap over the ridge, as this was the only way back to camp. It was midnight when we reached the pass, snow up to the belly of the horses. We were wet and starting to get chilled. Finding camp was critical. With the high wind and heavy snowfall, visibility was zero, flashlights were useless. I was in the lead on Smokey and let him take over. When he stopped two hours later, I thought he must have lost the trail. I turned on my flashlight. We were at the door of the wall tent at camp.

Whenever I needed an extra horse, I borrowed Doc Sloat's white mare. I can't recall her name, but it could have been Leapin' Lena. She was a smooth riding horse, good on the trail, but cinch-bound. As you tightened the cinch, she would begin to shake, sit down on her rear, and then leap straight up into the air. This was repeated two or three times before she stopped, then you could finish cinching. The remainder of the day, she would be fine.

Keith Hawn, prior to his becoming captain of the *Jolly Green Giant*, wanted to make a trip into the Independence Lakes near Albion. I assured him I had a good trail horse he could ride. I'm not sure, but I don't think he had ever ridden a horse in the mountains. We unloaded the horses from the trailer and Keith asked me which one he was going to ride. I told him the white mare.

I got Smokey saddled and was preparing to pull the latigo tight on Lena. I told Keith to get an axe handle out of the back of my truck. He wanted to know what it was for. I said it was a special saddling tool we needed for his horse and when her back legs start to buckle and she's going down, whack her across the ass with the axe handle. Minutes later she was cinched up tight and I said, "Let's go." Keith's response was something to the effect that, "If you think I'm going to get on that horse now, you're crazy as hell." Keith spent the remainder of the day on Smokey with both hands in a death-grip around the saddle horn. By the middle of summer, all I had to do when cinching Lena was lay the saddling tool on the ground in front of her.

Trail Spooks

What may appear to you as an object posing absolutely no threat can stampede even a seasoned mountain horse or mule. It is therefore extremely important that you always ride in the ready position: balls of your feet solid in the stirrups and excess slack out of the reins. When something happens, it will be instantaneous, you do not have time to get set for it. If you were thinking about what lures you were going to use when you got to the lake, hanging loose in the saddle, reins drooping when the trail spook jumped out, you could end up combing pine needles and manure out of your hair. Here's a list of common trail spooks found throughout the Rocky Mountains that you should watch for:

Black logs
White logs
Stumps (very bad)
Sharp noise
Dull noise
White rocks (very bad)
Dark rocks
Large rocks
Small rocks
No rocks

My mules have spent enough time in the mountains that wild animals do not seem to concern them. I have ridden them right past bull moose, elk, deer, coyotes, rattlesnakes, and black bears with little more than a casual glance. I was beginning to think they were completely fearless until one day a spruce grouse walked out in the middle of the trail in front of Sue, fanned out his tail, and challenged her to take one more step. Here was a ball of feathers that weighed less than eight ounces taking on 1,300 pounds of mule with a rider armed with a 30.06 rifle, .357 magnum revolver, and a double-bit axe. But, Sue refused to go on until the bird finally strutted off into the woods. With a large enough flock of these grouse, you could conquer the world.

I was packing fish one summer into some high lakes in the Boulder Mountains north of Sun Valley. About four miles up the trail on the side of a mountain, we came around a sharp bend, and there was a fourteen-foot aluminum canoe sitting on a two-wheeled hand cart. To say it was a bit of a challenge getting a packstring around the canoe would be a gross understatement. However, since this was the only time I have seen one of these on a trail, aluminum canoes are not included on the Spook List.

Ike and the Killer Stump

All horses and mules have a congenital fear that somewhere out there—they don't know which one, when, or where—the Stump will get them sooner or later.

Ishawooa Creek, Wyoming, September 30, 1990: When we got back to camp, Wes tied his horse Ike to what appeared to be a solid, tall lodgepole stump. The stump roots, however, were rotten and when the horse pulled back, the entire thing broke off at the ground and fell on him. Ike's worst nightmare had come true. The higher he jumped, the higher the Killer Stump leaped after him. By the time I got there, the stump had won and had Ike on the ground with all four feet in the air, lead rope twisting his head over his back, completely immobilized, waiting to be devoured.

IKE and the KILLER STUMP

The Stump Response

This stump response is a hereditary survival gene that can be traced back thousands of years when the horse was prey species for ice bears and sabre-toothed tigers. Only the animals that jumped and shied away from ominous shapes survived. It is a dominant gene that is also passed on to mules. Thus the stump response is triggered whenever a large black stump, or even a small brown one, appears suddenly on the trail.

Early Warning System

A mule's ear is a very sensitive piece of equipment. It constantly receives and sends messages. The smart rider or packer pays attention to the transmissions.

- Both ears to the rear and laid flat means: "Someone or something is about to get kicked, bit, or bucked off."

- One ear locked to the rear and the other rotating to the front and back means: "I'm checking out what's going on up front and behind as well."

- Both ears forward and locked means: "I'm really concerned about what's ahead." It could be a deer, elk, bear, or spook. If the mule suddenly stops in this ear position, be ready for a possible fast retreat to the rear.

- Neither ear locked in any position and both ears flopping back and forth means: "Ho-hum, nothing for a mule to get up-tight over." The rider or packer is cautioned not to assume the same attitude, since these conditions can change quite rapidly.

A horse has a much smaller ear than a mule, and does not have the range nor sensitivity of the larger mule ear. Horses tend to transmit similar signals with their ears, but will often leave the transmitter switch in the off position, and you won't get the message until it's too late.

Fish Cops

Pat was sitting on a rock trying to shake the water out of his ears. A few minutes earlier, an unnamed rapid on the South Fork of the Boise had flipped his raft over with the same ease a camp cook turns a sourdough pancake. I asked him if he had similar luck with riding his horse, because the following week, Pat, Dave, and I were scheduled to take a seven-day enforcement patrol with mules and horses into the Sawtooth National Recreation Area. His reply was, "I don't ride a horse, I have an Appaloosa mare." A small knot began to form in my stomach. I have had some unpleasant experiences with both Ap–paloosas and mares.

It was early afternoon by the time we got all the loads mantied* and ready to pack on the mules. Pat had brought along another mare in addition to his Appaloosa that he wanted to try out as a packhorse,

---

*A "manty" or "Manta" is a seven foot by seven foot untreated canvas used to wrap cargo for packing on horses and mules.

enlarging the knot in my stomach even more. I loaded her and the two mules, saving Coco until last. Coco had somewhat of a reputation, acquired the previous summer when I was breaking her to pack on a trip up the Queens River. She was very efficient in demolishing several pack loads as well as applying some mule tattoos to my body. I tightened up the cinch on her new Decker packsaddle, scratched her between the ears, and gave her a big kiss on the nose. Never kiss a mule on the lips. These days you could pass something on and make them sick. We started at the trailhead on the Middle Fork of the Boise above the mining town of Atlanta. To the best of our knowledge, the alpine lakes along the watershed divide, between the Middle Fork and the South Fork of the Payette, had not been checked by Fish and Game for perhaps ten years or more. This was a game warden's dream trip: virgin territory and crime running amok. Officers Pat Cudmore and Dave Cadwallader couldn't wait to get there.

It was now two in the afternoon and fifteen miles left to ride to the mountain meadow where we intended to set up a base camp. I was certain we could make it before dark, but had not taken into account the Appaloosa and the other mare. Two miles up the trail we stopped to adjust a packsaddle pad. Pat thought he had tied the two mares securely, until we saw their broomtails disappearing back down the trail at a high rate of speed.

Dave took off after them in hot pursuit. His horse, Barney, was getting a little excited part way through the race, so Dave decided he'd better stop, have a little talk, and calm him down. Barney wanted to race, not talk, so as soon as Dave got off, Barney let out his clutch and was gone, minus Dave. Now there were three horses charging down the trail to see which one could get back to the trucks first. We don't know which one won the race, but an hour later, Dave, on foot, returned to Go, did not collect $200, and once more left the trailhead with the horses. By now I suspect he too had developed a knot in his stomach.

We planned to check thirty-three lakes, riding some ninety miles of trails. Fifty-three people were interviewed, mostly backpackers, twenty-five miles from the nearest road. The backcountry telegraph is amazing. Within two days we began to encounter groups that would say, "Oh yeah, we heard Fish and Game was crawling all over up here." So much for the element of surprise. Pat and Dave didn't write a single ticket.

Hot Pepper Halter Rope

We have a mule that eats halter ropes like they were spaghetti. At fifty cents a foot, that gets to be pretty expensive mule feed. I decided I would put a stop to this habit during a Selway elk hunt one year.

After tying the mule up for the night, I painted cayenne pepper paste on the entire halter rope.

At daybreak I happened to look out the door of the tent in time to see a mule trotting by with six inches of rope dangling from his halter, headed for the creek and probably an urgent drink of water. That night I peppered another rope and slipped a length of plastic garden hose over it for extra protection. The following morning the mule trotted by again, headed for the creek, with six inches of halter rope/ plastic garden hose dangling under his chin.

After two seasons and seventy-two feet of halter ropes, the final solution was a chain. The cayenne is reserved for the chili.

Camp Entertainment

Camp entertainment takes on many forms, often involving one of the mules to provide us with some kind of excitement. One morning, Tom decided he would try his hand at entertaining us before breakfast. This was to be a demonstration of how to remove whiskers without shaving (along with a quantity of eyelashes and eyebrows). In order to do this properly, you squirt quite a bit of lighter fluid onto a reluctant smoldering fire, allow adequate time for the fluid to vaporize, and then throw a lighted match into the sheepherder stove with the door wide open, as you look inside to see if it's going to take or not. Fortunately, Tom was not injured and the stove did not exit through the side of the tent. His only comment, after the soot and ashes settled, was, "I think she'll take now."

One afternoon, John entertained us with some mule trick riding. His mule, Comin, as mules often do, decided on his own the best route through a thick growth of lodgepole pines. A small lodgepole, about four inches in diameter, had fallen horizontally between two trees with just enough clearance for a mule to go underneath, minus a passenger. Mules are very adept at judging minimal clearances. Rein pulling and the Universal Command failed to divert or slow Comin, once he had made his route selection. John grabbed the tree with both hands as it caught him across the chest, brushing him flat on the back of the mule. Comin then walked out from under him, John sliding off backwards over the rump, feet up in the air. John was still holding on to the tree as he cleared the mule when the pole bent and slowly let him down to the ground. I had never seen that trick done before and didn't know how to score it, but I gave him a nine for effort anyway.

Comin was also the "entertainment chairman" on our Washakie Wilderness sheep hunt in Wyoming. The weather at our spike camp, elevation 9,960 feet, was not good—hurricane force wind gusts, a foot of snow overnight, and no sign of the bad weather stopping. Feed for the mules was buried, so we packed up and headed down to base camp. Scoria Creek trail was bad enough when dry, but now it was soft, muddy, slick, and covered with a foot of wet snow. The head of the ravine was definitely impassable with the mud and snow.

The only detour available was a forty-five degree slope above the upper end of the ravine. I led Sue down first, tied her at the bottom, and was climbing back up to get the next mule. For some reason, Comin was loose, headed down the snow-covered slope in my tracks, gaining momentum. By the time he got to me, it was apparent that he didn't need or want any assistance. I had a choice of getting knocked off or jumping off the trail. Turned out to be a little bit of both. I landed on my back in the snow. The combination of plastic rain gear, snow, and a forty-five degree slope was comparable to hooking a ride on an Olympic bobsled. I wasn't too concerned about my descent as there was a grove of small lodgepole saplings about three feet in height that should have stopped me. I plowed right through them without slowing a bit. There was only one tree left. I grabbed it with one hand as I slid by and stopped, my legs dangling over a fifteen-foot drop into the rock-filled ravine. Unfortunately, Comin was the only one to witness the play of the day.

C'mon Stace, quit fool'n around.

In case you are wondering how Comin got his name, Wes had purchased one of two mules owned by Gary Gadwa, the conservation officer at Stanley. The names of the mules were Comin and Goin. Wes thought he had gotten Comin and that's what we called him for the next eight years. Actually he was Goin; the poor mule must have gone through a terrible identity crisis. He didn't know if he was Comin or Goin. He finally adjusted to his name change and no longer gave me puzzled looks when I called him.

Geographic Names

After being in the mountains for several weeks, you run out of reading material and things to do. Even the mules get bored and quit acting up. You have to resort to things like standing in front of a Coleman lantern at night and casting fifty-foot shadows against the trees around camp. Or, you can pull out a map of the local area and check out the various names.

Famous personages show up on maps, like Mt. Borah, an early Idaho senator, and the Frank Church Wilderness, another senator who helped craft the wilderness designation. The way the system works in naming geographic features after a person is that you usually must be deceased, and better yet, you should be a dead politician. You can take that any way you want to.

Some names did not require a lot of imagination. There must be hundreds of Deer Creeks, Rock Creeks, Dry Creeks, Warm Springs Creeks, Indian Creeks, etc., all over the West. On the Middle Fork of the Salmon, Horse Creek tributaries are logically named: Colt, Pinto, Filly, Bronco, Cayuse, Roan, and Broomtail. Pistol Creek, of course, has all the gun calibers and manufacturers. The ones I would like to know the history on are Hungry Creek, Starvation Point, Deadman Saddle, Rattlesnake Spring, Disappointment Creek, Phantom Creek, Dismal Mountain, Runaway Point, Arctic Point, My Creek, Our Creek, Dead Mule Peak, and Horse Heaven, to name but a few.

I do, however, know the source of the name Vinegar Hill on Big Creek. On July 30, 1879, a mounted infantry company of forty men, two of whom had been seriously wounded in an ambush the previous day, were surrounded by Sheepeater Indians. Their only protection was rocks and the cargo they had unloaded from the pack mules. The Indians set fire to the mountain, and only a change in wind direction saved the soldiers from being forced out of their refuge. The men had no water with them, and there was none available on the dry, rocky mountain slope where they were pinned down. During the night, some of the soldiers became so thirsty they resorted to sipping from a jug of vinegar they found in the supplies. From then on, the mountain was known as "Vinegar Hill." The company finally made its way back down the mountain to safety at 2:00 a.m. on July 31 under the cover of darkness. Their retreat from the Big Creek area went without further incident, except for the loss of sixteen pack mules.

A Box of Soup

No Name Creek (yes, it is on a map), Chamberlain Basin, September 9, 1991: We were part of an undercover enforcement effort, prior to the opening of deer and elk season in Frank Church Wilderness, that involved nearly every conservation officer, horse, and mule in the region. We had spent two days on the trail packing supplies to our campsite on No Name. The project had been so secret that even the Forest Service guard station at Chamberlain thought we were illegal outfitters and reported us to the Outfitters and Guides Board, who sent in a special investigator. We dubbed the operation the No-Name Outfitters, Inc.

The first night in camp, things were a bit disorganized, and Don Wright, regional conservation officer who was to be camp cook for the first two weeks, did not know where all his groceries were. I happened to have some fresh green beans Barb had given me from her garden and a stick of hard salami in my saddle bags. The only other grocery item that Don could find was a large box of dried Lipton noodle soup that he mixed up with the beans and salami. People tend to take for granted everything they use or consume with no thought as to the effort it took to provide it. However, Gary Loveland, Boise conservation officer and camp philosopher, put things into perspective for us: The box of noodle soup was picked from the shelf and placed into a shopping cart at a grocery store in Boise; the cart pushed to the check-out stand; taken out and run through the price scanner; placed back into the cart; the cart pushed to a truck in the parking lot; placed into the truck and driven to the Region Three office; taken from the truck to the storage room; taken from the storage room several days later and trucked 130 miles to my home in Lake Fork; stored in my shop and then loaded into a pack box; pack box weighed and trucked to the McCall Airport; loaded into a Cessna 206 and flown sixty miles into Chamberlain airstrip; offloaded and piled with a mountain of gear and supplies that was loaded on a Decker packsaddle and carried by mule to the No Name Creek campsite of a bunch of hungry game wardens.

But that's not all that was involved in the box of soup, since the mules also played a role. I drove 110 miles from Boise to pick up the seven mules; caught them in the pasture; loaded them in the trailer; drove back to Boise and picked up more gear; headed for Lake Fork but blew out a radiator hose; drove back to Boise for a replacement hose; then 100 miles north to Lake Fork; unloaded the mules late that night and tied them to a picket line; loaded them back into the trailer the following day and drove sixty-five miles to the Smith Creek trailhead and unloaded them; the next day the mules were loaded and spent eight hours on the trail climbing over Mosquito Ridge—with a fantastic panorama of the River of No Return—before reaching a campsite at Crane Meadows.

That evening in camp, Scott Reinecker, conservation officer at Yellowpine, decided to try out a set of hobbles for the first time on one of his Appaloosas. With the front feet hobbled, the horse began to run with its back legs while holding the front legs stationary. Once the rear end gained momentum, the Appaloosa began doing somersaults, rolled up into a huge spotted ball, and crashed into the timber 100 feet away. It missed going through our tent by about two feet. That would have been something to see—a ten by twelve wall tent with a hot sheepherder stove wrapped around a rolling Appaloosa.

We still had ten miles to go the next morning from Crane Meadows to Chamberlain airstrip. Brent Hyde, district conservation officer from Emmett, led off on his mule Cecil (possibly named after a prominent Idaho politician). At the first small stream crossing, Cecil sank belly deep into a hidden bog. I was right behind and only able to get half of my string of six mules across before they broke off. If Skeeter hadn't been carrying pack boxes that functioned like water wings, he probably would have disappeared. I had to find a narrower crossing that the remaining mules and horses could jump across. Nearly five hours later we arrived at the airstrip and began packing gear and supplies (the Lipton's noodle soup) to No Name Creek.

After supper I turned several mules loose to graze near camp, including Coco with a large bell around her neck. Later in the evening I tried without success to catch her so I could tie her to the picket line. She wouldn't even come to a bucket of oats, and took up residence for the night behind the sleeping tent which housed Wright, Loveland, Hyde, and Reinecker. Periodically during the night, Coco would shake her head, ringing the bell ten feet away from the tent. I think she was trying to awaken Brent to keep him from snoring so she could get some sleep. My tent was across the creek where I couldn't hear anything but the bubbling water. I was informed by the crew at breakfast that if I didn't catch Coco before dark and get the bell off her, she would be stew meat. I'm glad I caught her, because I don't think she could have competed with Lipton's noodle soup.

By the time the soup was ready to eat that evening, we had all gained a new appreciation for what it takes to produce a hot meal in the backcountry. Not a single noodle was left in the pot.

You'll Get a Kick Out of This

There was a pack string tied to the hitching rails at the Chamberlain Forest Service guard station, and two men were unloading a mule. All three disappeared in a cloud of dust—there's always a cloud of dust in these situations. As the visibility improved, I could see one of the men lying on his back some distance behind the mule. It seems the mule had been standing on the pack rope with his hind foot. But instead of pushing the mule over, the man kicked its leg with his boot so the mule would pick up his foot. The mule gladly obliged and slam-dunked the packer into the brush. Then to add insult to injury, I found that they had failed to leave evidence of sex on their elk and I wrote them a ticket.

My saddle mule, Sue, has a kick-dance routine she does at the beginning of every new trip. This can be unnerving if you're not used to it, so I'm the one who usually gets to saddle her. She's been doing this for years, but has never laid a hoof on me. If she really wanted to, she could have knocked off both my knee caps long before now—a mule can deliver a kick with any foot with crosshair precision.

The first time I used spurs on Comin when I was breaking him to ride, he reached up with his hind foot and spun the rowel. I thought, "He can't be that good with his feet," so I spurred him again; he spun the rowel again to show me it was no accident.

A couple years ago, Governor Cecil Andrus and a Fish and Game commissioner were attempting to load a fresh-killed elk on a mule that had never packed meat. This mule should be in showbiz. She hit the governor between the eyes with her front foot while nailing the commissioner in the head at the same time with her hind foot. Both of them rolled down the mountain, knocked colder than a mackerel, heads split open. It was highly unusual for a mule, being a party symbol, to assault a Democratic governor. She must have changed her political affiliation.

Coming Out of Chute Number...

Anyone who has made more than one trip in the mountains with saddle stock has had the opportunity to observe or compete in a sidehill rodeo. These are a lot more exciting than the ones you pay to see, especially if you are the participant.

Let 'er buck

Bill Fonshill, now of Boise, grew up in New Jersey. His wilderness connection came in the form of reading hunting stories in magazines like *Outdoor Life, Sports Afield,* and *Field and Stream*. His lifelong fantasy was to go on a wilderness pack trip with horses and shoot a trophy elk. Bill and I had done some deer and mountain goat hunting together, and he always talked about his dream hunt. One year, Wes and I decided to make Bill's dream come true and took him to the Selway.

Bill had had little opportunity, growing up in New Jersey, to gain much experience riding horses in the mountains. (If there had been a method of cloning horses, Smokey would have been one to clone; Bongo another.) Bill and I were doing some scouting the day before the season opened, riding down a really steep section of trail, when I heard Bill say, "Stace, could you hold up for a minute?" I looked back and Bill was upside down with his arms wrapped around Bongo's neck, both feet still in the stirrups of the saddle, which was now under the belly of the horse. Bongo gave me a look that said, "Will you do something about this?" Bongo never moved while I extricated Bill from saddle and horse. Bill had hunted hard without success for a week, and we were going to break camp the next day. It was still dark as we climbed the ridge trail on Stripe Creek. I heard a bull elk bugle down below us and stopped. Bill was bundled up like an Eskimo and hadn't heard anything. I pulled him off his horse, told him to hike for fifteen minutes down the mountain and blow his elk bugle when it got light. When we heard him shoot, we would come and pack his elk out. He stumbled off into the darkness, mumbling something like, "Yeah, right."

A short time after daybreak, we heard shots and went to look for Bill. Wes found him in a clearing, sitting on top of a six-point bull, holding onto the antlers like the handlebars of a motorcycle. All he could say was, "Take my picture! Take my picture!" I now had four elk, one deer, and the camp to pack out the following day.

On the ride out, Bill was riding on Bones and had pulled out his camera for a picture of the packstring going up the trail. We were on a steep sidehill, fifty feet above the Selway River. The click of the camera shutter might as well have been an exploding hand grenade. I heard a yell and looked back to see Bill the focal point of a rodeo. I hollered, "Get off on the uphill side," as both horse and rider disappeared. By the time I got back to the rear of the packstring, the horse was climbing back out of the river to the trail and a short distance behind was Bill on his hands and knees. I asked him why he hadn't gotten off on the uphill side. He said that he had, but by the time he cleared the saddle, it was the downhill side.

Appaloosas, Ed, and Lost Trails

As goofy as Bones acted at times, I think he was part Appaloosa. I don't mean to imply that this is a character flaw of the breed. It is the official state horse, and after all, I've also known some pretty goofy people over the years. The Appaloosa originated with the Mongols in Tibet, eventually was brought to Europe, ultimately sailed with the Spanish armada and joined the pillage of Mexico prior to 1600. By the mid-1700s, the Nez Perce Indians had acquired them and bred the Appy into a horse superior to all others in western North America. Chief Joseph and the Nez Perce were captured in 1877 after eluding the U.S. Cavalry for eight months in the mountains of Idaho, Wyoming, and Montana. The Army then confiscated, or rather stole, all their Appaloosa horses, and the breed nearly disappeared.

September 13, 1981: We had reached the end of the road down the Salmon River, at the Corn Creek Campground. Travel beyond this point was by foot, horseback, or boat. Wes wanted to hunt elk around Butts Point, which meant moving ten head of horses, gear, and five people across the river. Since I was the only one of the group with boating experience, I was elected to operate the oars on a small rowboat.

None of the horses had ever been in water over their knees. They had to be led into the river and individually pulled across behind the boat to keep them from drifting downstream into a set of rapids. The Appaloosa that Wes had borrowed was halfway across the river before she realized that her nose had to be out of the water in order to breathe. I was concerned that she was going to drown and drag the boat and me into the rapids before I could cut her loose.

I should buy some earplugs.

I had rowed over and back twenty times just to get the horses across the river, was hot, sweaty, tired, and beginning to develop a bad attitude. A lady from the nearby Forest Service campground, walking her dog, stopped and asked, "Why are you swimming those horses across the river?" I answered, "Because there's no goddam bridge." Luckily she didn't sic her dog on me, and if she ever reads this book, I apologize for being so short with her. It was 4:00 p.m. by the time the pack horses were loaded, and we still had 5,000 feet in elevation gain and 100 switchbacks to reach Butts Point.

We didn't know the name of the Appaloosa, but I was soon calling her Whirlygig. She had her own personal list of trail spooks that was as long as my arm. I never did figure out what any of them were. As soon as she saw one, she would do a 180 so fast that when you got her stopped, your hat would be twisted around in the opposite direction. Early one morning she got spooked, pulled the hitching rail loose, and tried to level camp with it before I caught her.

Wes had invited Ed on his first elk hunt. I sent him down a ridge with my elk bugle after a bull that had been talking back to me. My instructions to him were to be sure and blaze a trail on both sides of the trees from the elk, if he got one, as he came back to the main trail. We heard shooting at sundown and rode back up to where I had left him. Ed emerged from the woods at dark, informing us that he had killed a four-point bull.

Ed had gutted the elk and left it lying on the ground. The weather was unseasonably warm. We had to skin and quarter and hang it up, otherwise the meat would be spoiled by morning. I asked Ed where his blazes began. He said he didn't need to cut blazes because he knew right where the elk was, "in kind of an open spot by a log." How many places in the Frank Church Wilderness do you suppose would fit that description? An hour later, I went on point. I could smell the elk, which have a distinctive odor, and followed my nose uphill right to it.

It was near midnight as we started to ride back to camp. After Whirlygig had walked off the end of three switchbacks, it was obvious that she was totally blind in the dark. I had to get off and lead her the five miles to camp, like a seeing-eye dog. At least the trail spooks weren't bothering her any now, because she couldn't see a thing.

Our next hunt the following year was in the Selway Wilderness. The Appaloosa was not invited, but for some reason Ed and his father-in-law, Burke, were. Burke was a retired Air Force officer and wore one of those flight suits with pockets everywhere, during the entire trip, including inside his sleeping bag. Each pocket was stuffed with some emergency military ration, granola bar, flashlight, map, compass, signaling device, matches, or knife in case he got lost. This was hardly likely since he never got more than ten feet from the trail or left camp unless one of us was with him.

Ed would at least hunt alone and one morning shot a six-point bull elk. By the time he had it quartered and hung up, it was getting dark. Bad news for Ed because orientation in the woods, even in broad daylight, was not one of his strong points. He decided he knew exactly where the elk was and again did not make any blazes. Well, he sure didn't know where he was, walked all night long, and stumbled into camp the next morning at 5:30 a.m.

The following day, Ed insisted he could lead me right to the elk and I could easily pack it out with the horses. He said it was in kind of an open area near a small creek with a lot of small trees around. That really pinned it down. Four hours later, after climbing through downfalls, jumping logs, pushing through heavy brush, and wading muddy bogs up to the bellies of the horses, we rode out onto the top of a mountain. Ed, with a puzzled look on his face, said, "Something's wrong, there should be a creek here." My reply was largely unprintable. I turned the horses around and headed back down through the same mess to camp. We were actually two miles from the elk.

Wes had picked up Ed's trail from the day before and found the elk. For sixteen years, he and I had ridden up the Stripe Creek ridge and stopped, looking down into a place we called The Hole. It had to be one of the roughest areas on the upper Selway. We would blow our elk bugles and each time a bull answered back from The Hole. Wes and I would look at each other and smile, knowing that we'd never go down in there for an elk and have to pack him out. The bitter irony of it all, Ed had wandered into The Hole and killed the big bull.

Ed's Last Hunt

Selway River, September 1984: To classify this trip as an elk hunt might be stretching it, since it was more like a Wild West Show. Charlie Russell could have collected enough scenes to do paintings for a year or two. I should have anticipated problems with seven horses and four mules, half of which I had never worked with before. There was even a question about the ones I knew. Only recently had the bruises—compliments of Coco and a Queens River pack trip—healed.

Bones, who was scheduled to be my saddle horse, had blown up on two previous trips. I recalled a ride up the Butts Point trail, three years earlier, when Bones went bucking past me without anyone in the saddle. He had a thing about getting a lead rope up under his tail. A little farther up the trail, Act II, same script, plot, and action, except this time Bones and the pack horse ran off down the mountain scattering top packs and saddle bag gear as they went. They didn't go far and we found all the gear, although Wes felt and looked as though he had been run crosswise through a threshing machine. We topped out at Butts Point Lookout with an exploding red sunset that covered 100 miles of the horizon: All Idaho wilderness to the west and a huge orange full moon coming up over the mountains to the east. There was too much going on with the packstring to stop and take a picture. Besides, a camera could never have captured it anyway, but it's a picture that I will always remember.

I also recalled the previous year when Bones bucked Wes off again, rolled down the mountain minus Wes, and landed upside down in the creek, along with the remains of Wes's camera and rifle. Wes failed to see the humor in the water running into the muzzle of his 30.06 and out through the open breech. I had misgivings about riding Bones this trip, but Wes assured me they had roped cattle all summer with him and he should be okay. I was about to write a minority opinion.

The Selway River trail, after sundown, must rival a black hole in outer space—you are immersed in a sea of darkness. Bones had suddenly stopped and would go no further. I remembered that there was a big log across the trail, so I got off and led him over. I had climbed back into the saddle when Ed turned on a flashlight at the end of the packstring to see why we had stopped. If you are ever out at night with a string of mules and horses, please don't do this.

Bones took off bucking up the trail like he was in the national rodeo finals. I got him stopped after about fifty feet, but then he shifted into reverse and bucked backwards until he ran into the nose of the lead pack mule. He started forward again, this time doing 360s while bucking. By the way, horses have remarkable night vision, except for a couple Appaloosas I know. However, I wasn't convinced that Bones could see all that well or knew what the hell he was doing. In twenty-eight years of mountain trails and sidehill rodeos, I had never been bucked off—a record of which I'm proud and is probably worth several gold belt buckles. As Bones got into the bucking 360 degrees phase, I began to think my pride wasn't going to do me a whole lot of good under the circumstances. I take a long time to heal up anymore and wondered how to best make my exit. Flashes of light from the sparks flying off the horseshoes had revealed logs on one side of the trail and boulders on the other. My timing was flawless and I landed on my back in a pile of logs, though nothing was broken other than my twenty-eight-year old record.

We finally got everything unloaded by 11:00 p.m. and had the horses and mules grazing. There was time to relax in the tent with some of Sandy's elk stew. Then one of Ed's horses tripped over the A-frame holding up the tent. If my head hadn't stopped the ridge pole as it fell, the tent would have collapsed on everyone and the red-hot sheepherder stove, and we'd all have gone up in flames.

Two weeks and many rodeos later it was near the end of the hunt. Sandy and I planned to go out Friday with the elk meat. The rest of the group was to stay four or five more days and hunt. When they realized the cook and packer were leaving, they decided to go out with us. My back began to ache just thinking about it, because it meant getting up at 4:00 a.m., mantying all the gear and elk quarters, dismantling camp, and packing six horses and four mules. One of Ed's horses was left for six people to trade off riding. All this took until mid-afternoon and we had a twenty mile and eight hour hike to look forward to.

Gladys, the little black mule, was hooked onto Flash and at the first river crossing below camp, she went on the wrong side of a big log. The pigging string would have broken, except her lead rope had gotten hitched around the elk antlers that Flash was packing. Flash kept right on going, jerked Gladys off her feet over the log. She landed on her side in the river and was drug halfway across the river before the pigging broke. Gladys decided she wasn't going to take any more abuse and laid there submerged in the river with only her head sticking out and her ears folded down over her face like a black labrador retriever.

Wes waded out into the river and finally got her up on her feet without having to remove the pack load. She had on a sawbuck saddle with open-top canvas panniers (bags), which filled completely with water when she stood up. The panniers were old and full of holes, and she looked like a sprinkling truck as she staggered out of the river.

Until now, Ed had been riding his horse and asked if I would like to ride for a while. I said, "sure," because I knew there was a wide river crossing coming up and I wanted to make sure he at least got his feet wet. This was the first time I had been on this horse, and Ed failed to inform me that it was blind in one eye on the downhill side. We came around a bend in the trail and there it was. A Killer Stump. Instinctively, the horse jumped off the downhill side of the trail. Since this was his blind side, he did not know that it was thirty feet down, nearly straight off into the Selway River. For the second time this trip, I decided to forego the gold belt buckle and bailed off just as the horse was going into the water. I landed perfectly on my feet, like a cat. Sometimes I even feel like I have nine lives, but am uncertain which one I'm on now. I should find that out.

As I crawled back up to the trail, I was met by Ed, who informed me then that his horse was blind in one eye and he was concerned that he may have been injured. I could hear the horse bucking down the river and then crashing through the brush back up to the trail. I heard a moan and then everything was quiet. I went down the trail and there was the horse high-centered over a log with his head on the trail. I was happy to see this, because I was certain he should have a broken leg and I would have to shoot him with my .357. First, I was going to have Ed hold the head so I could shoot Ed in the foot at the same time. The horse apparently sensed I was going to blow his brains out, started flopping around, rolled off the log and jumped back up on the trail.

The rest of the crew talked me out of shooting Ed in the foot anyway, but only under the provision that he ride his blind horse out the rest of the way. I could think of several places on the trail where, if the horse sailed off again with Ed on him, I'd save some ammunition. When we got to the trailhead at 11:00 p.m., Wes walked up behind one of Ed's horses and it kicked him square in the groin. After that, he wasn't much help unloading the packstring.

Next morning we were standing around sort of glassy-eyed while Sandy was cooking breakfast and began relating our war stories from the day before. I discussed survival tactics when riding blind horses; Bones had pushed Ron off into the river; Eric had been drug down the trail by Coco after he accidentally poked her in the nose with his rifle barrel; Sandy had been on her hands and knees feeling for the trail along one of the cliffs after her flashlight quit; and Wes had a purple ring the shape of a horseshoe encircling his private parts. Everyone who walked the twenty miles had gotten completely soaked, ruined their leather boots, and blistered their feet. It was Ed's turn. He said, "Gee, I got charleyhorses so bad from riding, I had to get off and walk a couple times."

They had hidden my gun, so my only satisfaction was in knowing that this was Ed's last hunt. With any luck, maybe Bones and Ed's horses by this time next year would be gluing down flaps on letter envelopes and filling Alpo cans.

Missile Launch

Surprise Creek, September 17, 1989:

Moving kind of slow today and staying in camp. My left leg has turned black on the inside from my knee on up. The entire crotch is torn out of my Levi's. Yesterday we were riding down a ridge after scouting some 12 miles of high country for elk sign. I was test driving Skeeter for the first time and he had been doing fine. The next instant I was astraddle a Titan rocket missile headed for outer space. I had never before fully appreciated the G-forces associated with mule power-bucking. The thought that went through my mind was Maria telling me, "If you get hurt back there, you've only got another old man to get you out." During Skeeter's second launch, I conceded that the Universal Command was ineffective and wondered if the plastic Jesus on my saddle horn was going to pull me through. When we landed back on Earth, Skeeter's front legs buckled and his nose was in the rocks. I figured this was as close to the ground as I was going to be for a while, so both Jesus and I bailed off without waiting for the buzzer. Wes had been riding behind me and said Skeeter had gotten the end of a small, dead fir tree between his back legs, and the sharp end had speared him in a very sensitive portion of the male anatomy. I couldn't blame Skeeter for his reaction.

Forest Fires and Bladder Control

Red and I had gotten together only a few times over the years, and I wanted to take him on a mountain lake pack trip. I assured him it would be an easy trip in: a two-hour hike, some uphill but mostly downhill. I didn't explain that the "mostly downhill" was on the way back. A small effort would be worth the great scenery and outstanding lake fishing. We would be in the mountains for six days. The week before, I had packed in 100 pounds of oats for the mules, a tent, cook gear, and a picket line, and located a nice camp near one of the lakes. From here we could access five lakes containing brook trout, cutthroat, rainbow, brown, and grayling.

Conditions were extremely dry during the summer of 1994. Three wildfires in the Payette National Forest were out of control: Corral, Blackwell, and Thunderbolt. We had watched firestorms at night, ten miles away at the Blackwell fire, from my porch at home. I was concerned about thunderstorms that were forecast for August 11, the day we were packing in.

David and Mary Dudley came up the night before and helped weigh and balance all the packs. The rest of the group was Sue, Comin, Skeeter, and Simon. By noon at the trailhead, all the gear was packed on Skeeter and Comin, leaving two riding mules. Mary had bought feed for her mule, Simon, for a year and wasn't about to walk anywhere. I had to lead the two pack mules. I told Red that packers are restricted by Idaho state law from walking and therefore I was forced to ride in. Red and David took off on foot up the trail ahead of us.

Half an hour up the trail a thunderstorm hit and Mary and I put on our slickers. I had told Red I didn't think it was going to storm and to put his rain gear in the mule packs, since we hadn't had any rain for two months. Just in case, I showed him a rain jacket I had in my saddle bag for him. Slight problem: it was pouring down rain and Red was a mile up the trail.

It had quit raining by the time we caught up with them, so Red didn't need the jacket then anyway. The trail had steepened somewhat and Red appeared to be wilting just a bit. I told him to grab hold of Skeeter's tail and he would pull him right on up the mountain like a rope-tow at a ski lift. Red seemed hesitant about grabbing onto a mule's tail, especially one as big as Skeeter. I said, "No problem, we do that all the time." Red was carrying a walking stick. Skeeter apparently had a flashback to the time I was riding him in the Selway and a similar stick had jammed him between the hind legs. Red had barely gotten a grip on his tail when Skeeter expertly displayed the bottom side of his rear hooves along the sides of Red's hat brim. That apparently perked Red up some, as he decided maybe he wasn't all that tired yet.

We were riding up a ridge line, and Mary kept insisting she smelled smoke. I said, "Of course you smell smoke, half the state of Idaho is on fire." A few minutes later, Mary yells out, "Goddamit, I told you so, there's a f—— forest fire." It didn't take her long to develop a working vocabulary that both mules and mule packers could understand.

Well, sure enough, there was smoke coming from a spruce thicket down below us and I could see flames at the base of a big tree. We pulled a shovel and axe off a pack mule and rode down to the fire. Red was assigned to watch the pack mules while the three of us worked on the fire. This he was happy to do, as it could be done in a prone position. Two large spruce trees were on fire at their base and burning eight feet up the trunks. A large log on the ground was also ablaze. Both Dave and Mary are experienced firefighters and it appeared we would be able to control it. If not, our trip was already over.

We had three canteens, and fortunately there was a small stream nearby. While Mary was filling the canteens, I pissed into a hard-to-reach hot spot on the burning log. Who knows, that simple act alone may have extinguished another wildfire costing millions of tax dollars to control. The Chicken Peak Fire, ignited by the same storm on August 11, consumed 92,000 acres of the Payette National Forest and cost six million dollars in fire suppression efforts. The fires did not go out until snowfall.

After two hours of shovel, axe, and numerous canteens of water (I was only good for one piss), the fire was out. Dave decided to stay and watch it for another hour, just to be safe. Red had used the two hours to good advantage, allowing his body to heal for the final assault on what he was now calling The Rock.

I'll admit that the last pitch to camp could be classified as somewhat vertical. Red decided he was ready to grab a mule tail even if it meant being kicked to death. However, he did select Simon over Skeeter. This section of trail is like riding a mule up an extension ladder. Once they start, they can't stop because they will lose momentum and roll back downhill. Red was certain Simon's tail would come off as he pulled him up through the rocks. By the time we reached the first bench and stopped, Red's face was the color of his hair, and he was muttering something about "... some uphill, mostly downhill, all a bunch of lies." His recovery at camp took several beers and a cupful of George Dickel sourmash whiskey. After that he didn't seem to hurt much and was able to handle an elk steak dinner.

Dave was doing well in his new float tube and flyrod and kept us in fresh fish each day. Red hadn't caught a fish yet. All I had promised was great fishing, I didn't say anything about catching them. One day, Red applied lots of sunscreen so he wouldn't get sunburned, then he took off his shoes and socks so he could wade while fishing. By late afternoon, the tops of his feet were fried, and he was now concerned about being able to walk back to camp. We put him on Simon, so he was able to enjoy the scenery while ascending the rock ladder back to camp. A few beers and another cupful of George Dickel soon took the pain out of his feet.

Day number six on The Rock and time to break camp. Too bad, because Red was now acclimated to the high altitude, climbing mountains, and riding mules through the rocks. I was certain if we could stay another two or three weeks, he would even catch a trout. The pack out was pretty much routine, that is to say something was bound to happen. Riding a string of mules through several nests of yellowjackets is a sure way to liven up your trip, test your patience and riding skills, and expand your vocabulary.

I think, for the most part, Red enjoyed the pack trip, although there was a hint of dissatisfaction that surfaced one evening as we were recounting the fun we'd had. Red stated that when I died, he wanted me cremated so he could dump my ashes in the oat buckets. That way, the next time he made a trip to The Rock and saw a mule turd on the trail, he could give it a flying kick and say, "Don't worry, Stace, it's all downhill from here."

Afterword | The Missing Piece

ARLY IN OCTOBER 1996, John and I were once again packing mules, bound for Chamberlain Basin and a week of elk hunting. When you start getting closer to seventy years of age, you begin to wonder how many more of these trips you will be able to take. With a ten-hour mule ride through the mountains, there's a lot of time to contemplate this and look back on all the trips over the past forty-five years. Winter was always my favorite season. Hidden beneath a thick blanket of snow were the roads, stumps, trampled campsites, and litter of the previous summer and fall. Gone also were the people. The snow softened all sounds in the forest and at times it was so quiet, time seemed to stand still. You looked at your watch to make sure the second hand was still moving. This is how it was twenty years ago. Technology has changed all that. Advancements in outdoor equipment and winter clothing now bring people to the mountains year around. I guess that's not all bad, because these people have brought a new and powerful advocacy to preserve wild areas. Without them, much of our wilderness by now would have been exported to Japan.

As we rode, I tried to picture the high country meadows and ridge tops under ten feet of snow, marked only with the tracks of a pine marten or snowshoe hare. Wild Thing had taken me on many adventures down river canyons, through mountain blizzards, ski-climbing to the crest of the Sawtooths, and along several thousand miles of rocky trails just like this. Yet, each trip was somehow incomplete, the search never ended.

Around midnight, October 9, 1996, I was standing alone in the meadow beside the West Fork of Chamberlain Creek. The only visible light came from the northern array of stars, centered around Polaris; the only sound from the water in the stream as it moved and jumped over the rocks. Wild Thing had taken me by the hand and led me to this place. First came a low, deep howl, followed by another at a higher pitch. Then one after another joined in until an entire family chorus of wolves were singing their wilderness song, passed down to them for tens of thousands of years. I knew this was the piece that had been missing from all my years in the backcountry.

The song of the wolves was one of joy. Their search was over, they had returned. Their song was also one of sadness as they bid farewell to the chinook and steelhead that had filled this small, meandering stream since the end of the last ice age. Soon there would be another piece missing from the Idaho wilderness.

About the Author

STACY GEBHARDS was born in Illinois and spent his youth in the hardwood forests and on the Illinois River, hunting, trapping, and commercial fishing. Working on farms in the early 1940s provided training in the handling of horses and mules. By 1948, much of the wild lands of central Illinois had been decimated by strip mining for coal, forests cut for pulpwood, and the river silted and polluted by industries and raw sewage from Chicago and other river towns. Something said, "Go West."

Following a two-year tour with the Army in Germany and degrees in wildlife and fisheries management from Utah State, Gebhards began a career with the Idaho Department of Fish and Game that lasted for thirty-seven years.

Throughout his career he wrote articles, took photos, and gave presentations directed toward improving Idaho's water quality, protecting natural stream channels, preserving Hells Canyon and the Salmon River, and having the White Cloud mountains designated as wilderness. Gebhards engineered the language and helped pass the Idaho Stream Protection Act. Prior to retirement in 1993, he designed and constructed the stream complex at the Morrison-Knudsen Nature Center in Boise.

Official duties with Fish and Game and the attraction of Idaho's vast backcountry led him into whitewater rafting, kayaking, big game hunting, nordic skiing, and horse/mule packing. As he developed these skills he became a part-time licensed kayak guide and instructor, licensed backcountry ski guide, and a certified nordic ski instructor. He developed and taught training programs for Fish and Game personnel in kayaking, horse/mule packing, and winter mountaineering.

His publications include numerous articles, recipes, and photos for the Idaho Department of Fish and Game magazine, training manuals, and two illustrated handbooks, *Snow Snakes: How to Avoid Them* on cold weather survival, and *Mule School* on packing.